Unwanted Fraternity

UNWANTED FRATERNITY

An Authentic Journey Toward
True Healing After Loss

GREG
TONKINSON

NASHVILLE

NEW YORK • LONDON • MELBOURNE • VANCOUVER

Unwanted Fraternity

An Authentic Journey Toward True Healing After Loss

Published in New York, New York, by Morgan James Publishing. Morgan James is a trademark of Morgan James, LLC. www.MorganJamesPublishing.com

Proudly distributed by Ingram Publisher Services.

Morgan James BOGO™

A **FREE** ebook edition is available for you or a friend with the purchase of this print book.

CLEARLY SIGN YOUR NAME ABOVE

Instructions to claim your free ebook edition:
1. Visit MorganJamesBOGO.com
2. Sign your name CLEARLY in the space above
3. Complete the form and submit a photo of this entire page
4. You or your friend can download the ebook to your preferred device

ISBN 9781631957789 paperback
ISBN 9781631957796 ebook
Library of Congress Control Number:
2021919225

Cover Design by:
Rachel Lopez
www.r2cdesign.com

Interior Design by:
Christopher Kirk
www.GFSstudio.com

Morgan James PUBLISHING **Builds** with... **Habitat for Humanity** Peninsula and Greater Williamsburg

Morgan James is a proud partner of Habitat for Humanity Peninsula and Greater Williamsburg. Partners in building since 2006.

Get involved today! Visit MorganJamesPublishing.com/giving-back

To everyone who cared enough to share Jesus with Leigh Ann. She is rejoicing in heaven, and I will forever be grateful to you.

Contents

Introduction

March 6, 2010, started out like any other average Saturday for the Tonkinsons.

I'm forty-one years old. My wife Leigh Ann is thirty-five. We're thirteen years into an imperfect but overall good marriage. Our children, Caden, Bailey, and Malia, are ten, six, and four, respectively. We have two Shelties: Scooby-Doo and Scrappy-Doo. We live on a cul-de-sac. I'm wrapping up my second year as the Bible Department chair of a private Christian high school. Leigh Ann is on her twelfth year as a pediatric nurse at a children's hospital in town. I'm just finishing up my coursework for my doctoral studies and getting excited to begin writing my thesis. We are faithfully attending our local church and regularly meeting with our small group. Life is full, and life is good.

On that particular Saturday morning in March, Leigh Ann pulls out of the driveway in our 2005 Ford Taurus around six o'clock. She heads to the hospital for her twelve-hour shift. Even though I have the kids all day, it is far from burdensome. Spring break has begun, and we are more than ready.

The kids and I spend the morning at a nearby fair being put on by a local school. Caden and Bailey, the two boys, are full of energy, being helped, of course, by the cotton candy. Malia is finding her delight petting the small chicks and goats at the petting zoo. The afternoon isn't memorable, but it isn't terrible either. Dinner is whatever we can find in the refrigerator, which is typical when Leigh Ann works.

I know Leigh Ann's shift ends at 7:00 p.m., and I know it takes forty-five minutes to get home. It's not uncommon for Leigh Ann to arrive home from work somewhere between eight and nine o'clock. The kids are playing in the family room, and I'm watching a movie in the living room while letting my eyes scan their adventure in the other room.

Around nine o'clock, I send a text: *"Where are you?"*

The rest plays out like a movie.

There's a knock on the door at 9:45 p.m. Looking through the peephole, I can see a police officer with two other people, one on each side, wearing black windbreakers. None of them look happy. I open the door.

"Are you Greg Tonkinson?"

"Yes."

"My name is Officer Prather. I'm with Gilbert Police." He points to the others. "This is one of our child case managers, and this is our police chaplain. May we come in?"

I didn't want to seem like "that guy," but I've got young children in the house. "Can I see some ID?" The officer shows me his badge.

"OK. Come in." The four of us walk into the living room. I turn to the officer, "What can I do for you?"

"Mr. Tonkinson, is your wife Leigh Ann Tonkinson?"

"Yes, why?"

"Sir, you may want to sit down." I immediately began reviewing the last ten years of my life, wondering what I had done that warranted the police coming to arrest me on a Saturday night.

"If you have something to say, please just say it."

"I need to let you know, at approximately 8:30 this evening, your wife, Leigh Ann, was killed in a car accident. She was waiting at a stop light two miles from here and was hit from behind. I was first on the scene. Sir, we are so very sorry for your loss."

Eight thirty…wife…killed…car accident.

I never believed words could have physical weight. I do now. I hear those words, and my body collapses to the floor. I can't find my breath. Grief begins. I can only imagine what Caden, Bailey, and Malia are experiencing. Police, late at night, father collapsing in agony, now wailing. Terrified, they rush to my side. I am able to pull myself up to one knee, and the next few precious moments are what we now refer to as our *holy huddle*. I know the police officer, case worker, and chaplain are there with us, but it feels as if no one else is in the room. Just the four of us. They begin to cry, not fully knowing why their tears are falling. I can barely speak, but I manage to get out a few words.

"Mom was in an accident. She went to heaven tonight. And we're not going to get to see her for a really long time. We'll see her again in heaven, but for now it's just going to be the four of us. OK? It's going to be really hard, and we're going to have to be strong. She loved you very, very much." As the words left my lips, I still couldn't believe I was saying them.

Little did I know, while all this was happening, this unwanted experience was making its way to dozens of homes across town and around the country, waiting for people to hear the news and welcoming them into the fraternity. All of us will experience loss. Whether you're younger or older, male or female, Christian or Muslim, loss will come at a price. Yes, there are universal emotions experienced no matter how we lose someone. And to that end, my hope is that this book can bring some comfort to anyone experiencing loss.

But there is something unique about receiving *that* phone call, or getting *that* knock on the door, or being the first to arrive on the scene that is unlike any other experience. If that's you, I want you to know my heart breaks for you. You've been involuntarily initiated into a very select group: the Unwanted Fraternity. We are a coed fraternity of broken humans you may not have known existed. This is an unwanted initiation, one from which I'm sure each of us would gladly part if we could. But we can't. What happened in our lives cannot be undone.

I have been a part of this ever-growing fraternity for quite some time, and I meet more and more members every day. We share our stories with each other, we weep together, then we leave. And I selfishly rejoice after each encounter. Why? Simply put, you get me.

We're the ones who had weeks planned out that did not include picking out a casket, speaking with a funeral home director, or planning a funeral. We're the ones who had to look at young faces and, in an instant, summon the wisdom and courage to tell our precious children they'll never see their mother, father, brother, or sister on earth again. We're the ones who weren't planning on spending the next several weeks and months dwelling on worldview questions like, *Who am I in light of what just happened? What will the future hold? Where was God in all of this?* If you've entered into this unfortunate yet very special fraternity, this book is for you. You're why I wrote it. And my prayer is that God will show you there are many of us who need him and each other.

Chances are high we will never meet in person. But I believe you will discover that you and I have a lot in common simply because of our circumstances. Sudden loss creates shared experiences. After my wife's accident, there were countless nights of sleeplessness. And it was during those times when I thought I was alone in the dark that I found great comfort in both reading God's Word and reading books from other Fraternity members. These were people who deeply understood what I was feeling as if we were walking through my first year of loss together. I hope this book can be that for you.

Unwanted Fraternity does end with hope. But I do not want to formulate a false hope for you and guarantee something that may not happen. Nor do I want you to believe that your emotions and feelings will fall into place in a particular sequence. Emotions come and go with little warning or explanation. There will be days when you will both laugh and weep. There will be days when you will awake with a smile because you saw your loved one in a dream, but by midafternoon you'll be severely depressed. There will be days when you won't get out of bed, but somewhere in the monotony of lying there, you'll thank God for all he's blessed you with. You'll live many days in a paradox of doubt and faith. I want you know that I understand.

Hours after the accident, I began to journal. I'm not exactly sure why. Maybe it was because I had journaled before (though it had been years since I had any consistent entries). Maybe it was my way of dealing with things. Perhaps I had a moment of clarity in the newfound shock I was experiencing that allowed me to see the benefit of capturing my thoughts in real time so my children could one day read exactly what had happened. Regardless, journaling was what I chose to do, and I did it faithfully for one year.

This book is a compilation of those entries. *Unwanted Fraternity* encapsulates my first year of walking through the unexpected. Other than the first and the last, the ten themes named in the chapter headings are in no particular order.

In addition to my journal entries, you will see over 150 Bible references. This is by design. Early on in my journey I was advised that whenever you're in a conversation that matters, let God do as much talking as possible.

Finally, each chapter will conclude with an opportunity to connect with Jesus. I am a follower of Jesus Christ and have been for some time. I am a Bible teacher to young adults and regularly teach and preach to various audiences throughout the year. I will freely share my faith perspective throughout the book, as my faith provided so many resources during my times of pain. Jesus himself went through great pain and intimately understands our suffering. But by no means does having faith in Christ make one's journey easy. Rather, my desire is to pull back the veil to show my real struggles, how God journeyed with me through these struggles, and how my great loss ended up strengthening my relationship with God.

The Scriptures declare, "Therefore, since we have a great high priest who has passed through the heavens, Jesus the Son of God, let us hold fast our confession. For we do not have a high priest who cannot sympathize with our weaknesses, but One who has been tempted in all things as we are, yet without sin. Therefore, let us draw near with confidence to the throne of grace, so that

we may receive mercy and find grace to help in time of need"
(Heb. 4:14–16).

If you would not call yourself a Christian, my prayer is that you
too will find hope as well as learn more about Jesus and how he is
here for you. I would be honored to know *Unwanted Fraternity*
helped in some small way as you journey through your first year of
grief. But I would be infinitely more honored knowing this book
served as a prompt for you to run to Jesus with your pain. You'll
discover in these chapters Jesus truly does understand what you're
experiencing, and he has answers waiting for you.

Chapter One

Unquestionably Broken

I am weary with my sighing; every night I make my bed swim,
I dissolve my couch with my tears.
—Psalm 6:6

A Saturday in November on the East Coast is a perfect time to organize a tackle football game. Seizing the opportunity, I joined my neighborhood buddies at the local elementary school, three miles from my house. The air was cold, the ground was hard, and we were all ready to play as if pro scouts were in attendance. After a rather dismal first half, my team came up with a strategy that got us right back into contention. The score was now close and we were on the move.

As a junior in high school, I was 5'6" and proudly wrestled in the 98-pound weight class. Not exactly NFL material. But I was fast, so my position was wideout. And on this particular day, I was making a name for myself. Needing a score, my friend Ronnie drew up the play on the hard dirt—I line up on the left and run an eight yard down-and-in. We broke huddle, and I was feeling good about beating my defender to the inside with one of my patented jukes. Ronnie yelled hike, and I ran my route to perfection.

But as I looked back at Ronnie, I could see that he was in trouble. A defender had reached the universal five-Mississippi and had broken through the line, chasing Ronnie out of the pocket. As he rolled to his right, he could see I was open. But in order to get me the ball, he would have to rush the pass. With that as his only option, Ronnie let it fly. What came out of Ronnie's hand is what they refer to in football as a lame duck. The ball waffled and waved up in the air taking way too long to reach me. This allowed my defender to catch up, and when the ball finally reached me, so did he. All of him.

As we both fell to the ground, everyone heard a loud, deep crack. My femur bone (the thickest in your body) had split in half. At the time, I knew nothing about femur bones. Nor did I know the intense procedures I would be introduced to in the weeks that followed to regain full mobility in my leg. All I knew when I got tackled was something was unquestionably broken.

This was my first journal entry after I found out Leigh Ann was killed.

Day 0: Tonight, around 8:30 p.m., my life, my love, my wife, passed away. Sudden car accident, so I'm told. It's 1:13 a.m. now, and I'm awake but I'm dead. I can't believe I'm writing these words, yet all of them are true. Leigh Ann Tonkinson, my absolute love, the best mother to our kids, the best wife I could ever imagine, has left this earth and is in heaven. Every day, beginning with this one, will be a long day. I have our three wonderful children to keep me company until Jesus calls me home. Selfishly, I pray it will be tomorrow. Still cannot believe this is real. My wife has died. Three children lost their mother four hours ago.

The questions are endless. The pain is overwhelming. The hurt is all-consuming. I don't know what to do. How I sincerely wish it were me. Leigh would have done so much better at giving our kids a fighting chance. Now they're stuck with me. I don't know what it's like to live without a mother. Three kids will have to discover that. They will have to attend their mother's funeral. I wish that upon no one.

A thought to Leigh Ann—I know you're enjoying heaven and all that it has for you. I know you're not wanting us to suffer. But if you can get inside my heart right now, you'll see how much I love you. I miss you so much, honey. I miss everything about you. I am so sorry for the times I made you sad, the times you didn't like "us." I hate myself for that. I love you. I love you. I love your smile. I love your way with our children. I love your sincerity. I love your childlike faith. I love your intelligence. I love how you were so excited for my life. I love you. And right now, I miss you. My heart hurts and I want you back. I want you back from heaven so we can live out our years together. Just you and me. Please enjoy your new home. You're the love of my life. —Me

Unquestionably broken. This was evidenced by more entries, which I posted on a blog so others could keep up with what was happening in our lives.

Day 11: I can't describe the pain. Missing her has been harder and harder each day. I don't know how to live life waking up every day knowing I'll never hear Leigh Ann (on earth) laugh, talk, sneeze, ask brilliant questions, settle me down when I'm upset, argue (well) with me, say the most loving things to our kids. I'll never see her dance, swim, sit somewhere where she was just loving life (over at her mom's, by the pool, playing games, at church). I'll never see her out in the audience when I preach. The rest of my life will be lived each day with "I'll never…" And that reality has broken my heart. Quite torturous when you get up each day and your bleeding, tender, broken heart has to endure another round of abuse. Nothing compared to my Savior's torture, but I'm a wounded man and can't see any way out of it. My wife has been killed at age thirty-five. I'll spend my days without her. I can't believe it.

Day 21: Still settling into the fact that Leigh is gone. I can't believe it. I'm going through my days without her and there is such a massive void in my life. I am lonely beyond words and yet there are people all around me. The loneliness comes from missing just one person. I could meet one thousand people and if none of them are Leigh Ann then I'm still lonely. I need her. I need my wife. I need the one who I was supposed to spend years and years and years with. We were supposed to see our kids graduate, and date, and get married, and have children. We were supposed to be grandparents and enjoy playing with our grandchildren. We were supposed to travel and vacation and enjoy life together. We were supposed to enjoy ministry together. We were simply supposed to be together. No matter what else would happen in life we were supposed to be together.

Leigh Ann is dead and none of this will ever happen. I hate everything about her death. I hate empty closets. I hate knowing three kids will not have their mother. I hate every room I'm in that she's not in. I hate playing with the kids outside knowing she's not on the porch swing watching us. I hate thinking all the time about the future. I hate sleeping in the bed that used to be for the both of us. I hate not having her to tell my day to. I hate not having her to talk with in the car. I hate not having her to laugh with. I hate not being able to hug her. Leigh Ann is gone and I hate it.

Life is continuing to move on but I can barely get by because I can't bear the weight of what it means to live life without Leigh Ann.

Day 106: *My phone is set up in such a way that it keeps all my texts by way of "threads," so I can see all the conversations I've had with someone. As I happened upon Leigh's contact information, I started reading the last few days of texts we had sent to one another. I read what we talked about on March 1, 2, 3, 4, 5, and 6. In a moment's time, I was immediately taken back 106 days and was reliving the conversations I had with my wife. I could hear her voice through her texts as clear as if I were talking with her today. We talked about missing each other throughout the day and what our plans were going to be for the upcoming weekend. On March 5 Leigh texted me that she asked her mom to watch the kids so we could go clothes shopping and grab some dinner. After deciding to eat at Black Angus (one of Leigh's favorite restaurants) she texted, "Oh sweet, now I'm excited…" and I could just see her smiling and truly being* *excited to do some shopping and eat some steak. Neither of us knew that would be our very last "date." My last text on March 6 reads "Where are you?" I had no idea Leigh Ann had died and was already in heaven.*

One hundred and six days later and the tears fall as painfully as they did on day 1. All it takes is a little reminder, through a cell phone, that the person who meant the most to you is now gone, and your night goes from manageable to unmanageable. I had forgotten what Leigh Ann sounded like and it all came back to me. Now I miss her more than I've ever missed anyone.

Day 320: *No prayer requests or prayers, just a brief post tonight…If words carried weight, these next four would crush a small planet—I miss Leigh Ann. That may or may not mean much to anyone else and that's OK. I saw a picture of her today while I was teaching, and I was instantly brought to a place of missing my wife so very much. Life was right with Leigh Ann.*

Perhaps what makes this brokenness so painful is that it takes place mainly on the inside and the timing is unplanned. One minute you are doing life, and the next your mind is flooded with memories that leave you longing whether that be day 10 or day 300. At some point the pain subsides for a few moments, maybe even a few days, but then something triggers the pain and you're back to indescribable misery.

> **Perhaps what makes this brokenness so painful is that it takes place mainly on the inside and the timing is unplanned.**

Weeks after Leigh's death, a friend connected me to another Fraternity member, Jerry Sittser. Jerry is a professor, author, and speaker who lost his wife, daughter, and mother in a head-on collision with a drunk driver. Up until that phone call, I had never met Jerry nor had I read any of his books.[1] All that was told to me was that he was another widower who might be able to empathize. I called Jerry late one night and had a conversation I will never forget. As I shared my newfound grief with him, he not only empathized but also cried with me. Fellow believers, Fraternity members, brought together by tragedy, sharing a profound moment.

Among the many words of wisdom Jerry had for me that evening, one phrase stands out. He said that I will experience a range of unexpected and unwanted emotions in the months to come. And what I should anticipate feeling is what he called *internal chaos*.

He said, "It sounds like you've got your house in order. You've got plenty of family to help with the kids, you've got a good network of friends for support, you've got people helping with the everyday duties of life. So, externally, your life seems to be in good shape." And he was right. Arguably, my external life might have been in better shape than it was prior to the accident.

"But," he said, "I'll bet you're a wreck mentally and emotionally. That's what I call internal chaos. It's the stuff nobody else can see. It's the constant thinking about Leigh Ann, the wondering how you'll do life as a single father, the pain of losing your wife and now living alone, and the thousands of questions that will never be answered. People will gauge how you're doing based on if you've showered, if your house is picked up, if your bills are paid. They think you're OK if those things are in order, but they have no idea of the battle that's going on inside."

Those words brought tears to my eyes, not because I was sad, but because he was right and he understood. This is what it meant to be unquestionably broken.

The Scriptures don't shy away from letting us peer into the souls of others who were in internal chaos. God designed His Word with such simplicity that even my children could appreciate why we used a Psalm 23 plaque to decorate the casket or why John 3:16 is written out on Leigh's headstone. They read those powerful words and make a connection between God being Leigh Ann's Shepherd, or Leigh Ann being in heaven because Jesus died for her sins. But God also supernaturally illumined the writers of His Word so that they would capture the depths of brokenness for desperate souls who needed to see how others had handled their internal chaos, especially in light of their faith. Job and David come to mind.

Job (who receives my vote for Unwanted Fraternity president) faced loss like none other. This wealthy, God-fearing man began one of his days witnessing a servant running to him with the terrible news that the Sabeans attacked one of his fields, stole all his oxen and donkeys, and murdered all his servants. In an instant, Job experiences financial and relational devastation. He may have been thinking the worst had just happened. But while his servant was still speaking, another servant ran from afar to tell Job that fire fell from heaven and burned up all his sheep and the servants tending to the sheep. Job is faced with the reality that his feelings of loss can actually get worse. And the Scriptures declare that while Job is crushed by the news of his two servants, he sees yet another servant coming toward him. The Chaldeans made an attack on Job's camels and stole them while also killing all the servants.

Job was beginning to understand how painful life can be, but he hadn't even begun to reach the depth of his anguish. Not until the fourth and final servant approaches Job with the cataclysmic news that while his sons and daughters were eating and drinking at the oldest brother's house, a great wind struck the house and it collapsed, killing everyone, does Job realize what it feels like to have his soul crushed.

In the span of four conversations, Job has experienced complete economic ruin and devastating human loss. But we're not finished. As Job mourns, Satan smites him with sore boils from head to toe, Job's wife has given up on God and encourages Job to do the same, and Job's three friends console him by assassinating Job's character and blaming him. The mass destruction that took place in such a short period moved Job to curse the day he was born.

> Let the day perish on which I was to be born, and the night which said, "A boy is conceived." May that day be darkness; let not God above care for it, nor light shine on it. Let darkness and black gloom claim it; let a cloud settle on it; let the blackness of the day terrify it. (Job 3:3-5)

King David also encountered incredible amounts of pain and suffering. Chosen by God to be the second king of Israel, David began his illustrious career by besting the giant Goliath in a stone-versus-sword fight. The reigning King Saul, flooded with jealousy, made several attempts to end David's life. Affectionately known by God as "a man after My heart" (Acts 13:22), David spent over a decade fleeing from King Saul's attempts and would often turn to pen and ink to convey his feelings. Here are just a few.

I am weary with my sighing; every night I make my bed swim,
I dissolve my couch with my tears. My eye has wasted away
with grief; it has become old because of all my adversaries.
(Ps. 6:6-7)

I am poured out like water, and all my bones are out of joint;
My heart is like wax; it is melted within me. My strength is
dried up like a potsherd, and my tongue cleaves to my jaws;
and You lay me in the dust of death. (Ps. 22:14-15)

Save me, O God, for the waters have threatened my life. I
have sunk in deep mire, and there is no foothold; I have come
into deep waters, and a flood overflows me. I am weary with
my crying; my throat is parched; my eyes fail while I wait for
my God. (Ps. 69:1-3)

Other Fraternity members in the Bible experienced similar feelings as Job and David. Well-known characters like Abraham, Elijah, Jeremiah, Peter, and Paul went through occasions of loss and grief. Even lesser-known characters like the widow in Luke 7 who lost her only son, the ten lepers in Luke 17, the woman in Mark 5 who had a hemorrhage for twelve years, or Aeneas in Acts 8 who was bedridden for eight years experienced loss in some way. All are Fraternity members broken from circumstances that produced grief.

If you're unquestionably broken, you are not alone. That doesn't take the pain away, but it may help to know that hosts of people, including me, know what you're feeling. But more so, God knows what you're feeling, and though you may already know this, he's nearer to you right now than you know. David proclaimed this in

Psalm 34: "The Lord is near to the brokenhearted, and saves those who are crushed in spirit" (v. 18). Don't deny your brokenness, but please believe the next verse in that powerful psalm: "Many are the afflictions of the righteous, but the Lord delivers him out of them all" (v. 19). God is about the business of delivering you from your affliction. It will take more than a day or two. Maybe even a year or two. But take comfort knowing he's right there with you in your brokenness.

Connecting with Jesus

Jesus can relate to you in your brokenness because he too experienced loss. In fact, Jesus experienced loss more than once. Our Savior joyfully entered into a multitude of relationships while on earth. And just like in some of your relationships, some of Jesus's relationships ended abruptly due to unexpected deaths.

> *Jesus can relate to you in your brokenness because he too experienced loss.*

Jesus and John the Baptist, by most accounts, were cousins. Elizabeth, John's mother, and Mary, Jesus's mother, were relatives (Matt. 1:36) who were blessed by God to be pregnant at the same time, though Elizabeth was considerably older than Mary. Elizabeth delivered John in Judea, and about six months later Mary gave birth to Jesus in Bethlehem. We don't have many details of John and Jesus in their early years, but we're given front row seats to their public ministries and relationship with each other as adults.

John, the older cousin, humbly accepts the role of forerunner to Christ. Like the prophets Isaiah and Malachi, John's primary role was to "make ready the way of the Lord" (Matt. 3:3). John had quite a following, attracting even Pharisees and Sadducees who would come and listen to his message of repentance. He also had his own disciples, including Andrew and John, who left his tutelage to become disciples of Jesus (John 2:35–37). John had influence and reach, but he will always be remembered as the one who put Jesus before himself: "He must increase, but I must decrease" (John 3:30).

John suffered one of the most uncalled-for deaths recorded in all of Scripture. A spineless King Herod, who, at the demand of his wife Herodias, placed John in prison, gave in to the gruesome request of his stepdaughter and had John beheaded purely out of spite (Mark 6:14–29). When Jesus was told the news, "He withdrew from there in a boat, to a lonely place by Himself" (Matt. 14:13).

On another occasion, Jesus was informed his good friend Lazarus was sick. At this point, you've probably heard the rest of the story. Lazarus has been dead for four days; he's lying in a tomb wrapped like a mummy. Jesus tells his sisters to remove the stone in front of the tomb. Martha tells Jesus Lazarus will stink. And in dramatic fashion, Jesus yells for Lazarus and out comes a formerly dead man, stench and all!

This would be the last miracle Jesus would perform before his own death and resurrection. He used the death and resurrection of his good friend to show his disciples he has "abolished death and brought life and immortality to light through the gospel" (2 Tim. 1:10). Jesus was and has always been victorious over death!

So, why then do we have this exchange right before Jesus performs his miracle?

> When Jesus therefore saw her weeping, and the Jews who came with her also weeping, He was deeply moved in spirit and was troubled, and said, "Where have you laid him?" They said to Him, "Lord, come and see." Jesus wept. So the Jews were saying, "See how He loved him!" (John 11:33-36)

When Jesus experienced the loss of loved ones, he withdrew to a lonely place by himself, and he wept. Interestingly, the Scriptures only record three times Jesus wept, and this is the only occasion when it was for an individual other than himself. Certainly Jesus could have chosen other ways to express himself. But in these two instances, he seemingly acted very much like you and I would. Perhaps in his humanness, he was hurting and desperately needed to be alone with the Father. Perhaps he was reminded of how deep love can be when he saw loved ones wailing in grief, trying to catch their breath, only to wail more. Perhaps he was tired of how death can so quickly destroy. Perhaps he was unquestionably broken too. Could Jesus, in his humanity, have donned the Unwanted Fraternity insignia on his tunic? I believe so. In our very broken world that isn't a stranger to death and grief, perhaps Jesus, wrapping his mind around the infinite and finite all in one, stopped for a moment and let grief become a very real emotion. In his divine humanness, he related to his creation. And he wept too.

There is hope written in the very sacred words God has given us. One day death will be swallowed up where there is no more. Until then, Jesus knows your pain and wants to walk with you in it.

Chapter Two

Widespread Anger, Part I

*Be angry, and yet do not sin; do not let the sun go down on
your anger, and do not give the devil an opportunity.*
—Ephesians 4:26–27

I refer to what happened to Leigh Ann as an *accident* because by definition that is what it was—"an unfortunate incident that happens unexpectedly and unintentionally, typically resulting in damage or injury."[2] I do believe that term has become tired because of its overuse and misapplication. Today all of our mishaps and erroneous decisions are self-proclaimed "accidents." No one to blame, we're all human, mistakes happen. That is not how I'm using this word in reference to what happened to Leigh Ann. There was someone to blame. There was someone who killed my wife and the mother to our three children.

When the police arrived to break the news, I couldn't process the details. I couldn't get past the heaviness of "your wife was killed." Based on their strong counsel, I didn't leave the house and go to the scene. Part of me is glad. Part of me wished I had. I don't have any graphic images to replay in my head, but I will always feel as if I abandoned my wife in her time of need.

As the days passed, I spent a great deal of time thinking about the details of what had happened. Many who experience loss will look for objective answers. The facts of the situation won't bring our loved ones back, but facts do keep our minds from wandering. They serve as constants in times of chaos.

Early in the investigation into what exactly happened, I was told an off-duty officer witnessed the twenty-year-old driver who killed Leigh Ann run through two red lights before he drove into the back of her car. Leigh was coming home from work, waiting at a stoplight, when she felt the entire force of his vehicle hit her at an estimated speed of 75 miles per hour. Her car, now this knotted configuration of plastic and metal, was immediately launched into the dark sky only for a moment before it landed upside down in a nearby ditch. Leigh Ann was hanging upside down, still secured in the driver's seat when the first responders arrived. By their immediate observation, they knew she was already gone.

Because this accident had fatalities, autopsies were mandatory. A few weeks after the accident, I was given Leigh's autopsy report. I couldn't understand all of the medical jargon, so I asked my good friend, a pediatric surgeon, if I could send him the report so he could help me better understand how Leigh died. He and his wife knew Leigh Ann, and I knew I was putting him in a precarious position, but I needed answers. He graciously looked over the report and then sent an email that was prefaced with a heartfelt apology of what he discovered. He explained what had happened and did his best to comfort me by repeatedly stating her death was instant. But he could not deny the violence. Peppered throughout were statements such as "in all my years of taking care of patients (and I have seen a LOT of trauma), I have never seen this"; "she had a combination of numerous injuries—each of which could independently be sufficient to take someone's life"; and with injuries the kind Leigh experienced, "patients simply do not make it in from the field to us in the trauma bay." Simply stated, Leigh Ann's "accident" was brutally violent.

The facts I would receive in those first few weeks drew me down to places I had never before been. We've all experienced anger, maybe even rage, but when reviewing those moments, we struggle to justify how our emotions got the best of us. My emotions after the accident were different. They weren't irrational or unintentional. They were cold, calculated, and dark. Anger began to consume me, and I didn't seem to mind.

Day 3: I'm so mad at the kid who took my wife's life. This twenty-year-old who took a mother from her three children. I wanted to exact revenge on his family. Someone told me that he was the second child to die within a year and a half in that family from a car crash. I'm still angry with him. He's dead, and for me that's good only in the sense that I don't have to spend my days trying to chase him down and do unspeakable things to him. But I'm still angry with anyone who knows him. I know I can't be that way, but for now this is how I feel.

Day 16: Heart is breaking right now. Malia is reading the ABC book with Grandma Peggy as I work at the computer. I can hear

Leigh giggling with Malia and reading with her: "Big A, little a, what begins with A?..." Now Malia is singing the alphabet song—"A, B, C, D, E, F, G..."

Why in the world isn't Leigh Ann here to enjoy watching her daughter grow up? Why isn't she here to say, "Bedtime in fifteen minutes!" Why isn't she here to give me a hug or to let me rub her shoulders because she's worked hard all day? Why isn't she here?

She's not here and will never be here on earth again because she was waiting at the red light to come home. She was waiting to do all the things I just listed above. She was simply waiting.

All I know is that this kid got in his car and drove fast and reckless not just for a few moments, not just for a split second. He made a series of bad choices, one after the other, over and over again. For miles he drove without care. And then he plowed into the back of my wife's car so hard he broke her neck.

Don't tell me how nice of a kid he was. Don't tell me how we all make mistakes. Please don't ever tell me this is something we'll just have to learn from.

Leigh Ann lost her life all and only because this kid decided to get in his car and drive without care. Leigh Ann died because he killed her. Leigh Ann died because this kid became a killer and she was his victim. He may not have known her prior to the accident, but the second his car hit hers, he became a killer. I will forever know him as a killer.

Day 47: *She was hit by another car so hard that she died instantly and her car flipped on to its top. It wasn't neat and comfortable and pretty. It was horrific and ugly. I replay the accident in my head several times a day. My dislike for the other driver has not lessened. I have immense anger toward someone who drives so recklessly, especially since it has been concluded that he was not impaired with drugs or alcohol.*

At its core, anger is about revenge. It's deciding that what happened was wrong, and something needs to be done about it. It's playing the judge and jury whereby I get to decide how, when, and for how long someone must be punished. Even more so it's about feeling good when the punishment occurs.

> *At its core, anger is about revenge. It's deciding that what happened was wrong, and something needs to be done about it.*

Though I was aware of all of this, my anger toward the young man who killed Leigh Ann remained constant. I had nothing but contempt for him and his family. This person took so much from me and my kids. His actions were senseless. The damage he caused could not be undone. And for what? Why did he do this? There were no alcohol or drugs found in his body. And seemingly he wasn't driving somewhere that required him to drive at such a high speed. So why did this happen? What caused him to get in his car and make such bad choices? I will never know since he also passed away at the scene.

One thing that helped was knowing I wasn't alone with my feelings. Many friends and family joined me in my ire. Even those who saw things a little differently would remain silent knowing it was relational suicide to tell a newly titled widower he shouldn't dwell in such dark places. Being angry at this young man felt good. It felt right even though I was up against a host of competing Bible passages.

A man's discretion makes him slow to anger, and it is his glory to overlook a transgression. (Prov. 19:11)

A fool always loses his temper, but a wise man holds it back. (Prov. 29:11)

Do not be eager in your heart to be angry, for anger resides in the bosom of fools. (Eccles. 7:9)

But I say to you that everyone who is angry with his brother shall be guilty before the court; and whoever says to his brother, "You good-for-nothing," shall be guilty before the supreme court; and whoever says, '"You fool," shall be guilty enough to go into the fiery hell. (Matt. 5:22)

Be angry, and yet do not sin; do not let the sun go down on your anger, and do not give the devil an opportunity. (Eph. 4:26)

But now you also, put them all aside: anger, wrath, malice, slander, and abusive speech from your mouth. (Col. 3:8)

This you know, my beloved brethren. But everyone must be quick to hear, slow to speak and slow to anger; for the anger of man does not achieve the righteousness of God. (James 1:19-20)

Who wins out when our attitudes and actions disagree with the Bible? Could I stay angry at this young man? If so, for how long? Was I modeling for my children a Christlike response to tragedy? Where would forgiveness fit into all of this? And when would I have peace?

I've heard it explained that our anger is justified because God himself was frequently angry with the Israelites and Jesus cleared out the temple with a whip of cords (2 Kings 17:18; Amos 1:2; Matt. 21:12–13). Theologically, the above examples are known as acts of righteous anger. Righteous anger involves acting in anger without introducing sin (Eph. 4:26). There have been a few times in my life when I've acted with righteous anger. My anger toward the young man would not make that list, and I knew that.

I wish I could tell you I had an epiphany during that first year that caused my anger to vanish. But then I wouldn't have written this on day 323.

Day 323: Getting ready for bed I took the pillows off of Leigh's side and tossed them to the ground. I keep pillows on her side though they're never used. I instantly felt alone. The room felt larger than normal and more quiet than usual. It dawned on me that for over three hundred days no one has slept in our bed but me. That feeling triggered feeling angry toward the kid who killed Leigh Ann. I was instantly back at the funeral home looking at her in the casket trying to get a grip on the reality that she is dead. It was a senseless death and so I'm angry.

I was angry, some would say rightfully so. Maybe you're reading my story and you can relate, and my anger is giving you justification to live with anger. I want you to know I understand. But for me, during year 1, the more time I spent living with anger (which was often), the less time I was asking God to give me what I really needed—peace and the ability to forgive.

Something I chose to do at the end of each journal entry was write a prayer. As I read back through them, admittedly, they are some of the most honest prayers I've ever prayed. I expressed to God exactly what was on my mind, how I was feeling, and what I needed from him. I know the ACTS acronym (adoration, confession, thanksgiving, supplication) and understand the value of following this format. But these prayers didn't follow a set pattern. They were from a desperate, often angry man who was trying to remember the truths about the God he had known for over two decades. Embedded in many of those honest prayers were cries of anguish followed by petitions for peace.

> *Day 21: Father, I know your ways are good. I'm just not seeing that today. I'm not seeing how this is all going to work out. And honestly, I need Leigh back. I need my old life back. So please help me see you in the depths of this hurt. I need your peace.*

> *Day 54: Father, I'm broken, I'm tired, I'm full of your blessings, I'm in awe of your sacrifice for me. I'm both hurting and hopeful tonight. I wish I was just hopeful but that isn't my life right now. I pray for your presence to invade me with comfort and peace.*

> *Day 251: Father, it's another day where I need to be filled entirely with your peace. Another day where it's too tempting to get caught up in missing Leigh Ann. Thank you for the family and friends that are helping me make the most of today. Thank*

you for my kids who want to see me happy. May my joy be found in the Lord today.

Often, I found myself asking God for peace. Peace so I could parent. Peace so I could function at work. Peace so I could sleep. I wanted peace to replace the anger. In reading Philippians 4:6–7, I was reminded that through prayer and thanksgiving God will eventually bring me peace: "Be anxious for nothing, but in everything by prayer and supplication with thanksgiving let your requests be made known to God. And the peace of God, which surpasses all comprehension, will guard your hearts and your minds in Christ Jesus."

At times, though, it was difficult to see through my prayers of desperation.

This peace Paul talks about is real peace. Unexplainable, unimaginable, true-to-the-word peace. As the kids and I traveled through that first year without Leigh Ann, the only reason we kept moving forward was due to God granting us moments of this biblical peace. I wasn't ready to forgive the young man who killed Leigh Ann (that would happen a few years later), but I knew enough to know I couldn't keep waking up every day feeling angry. The kids and I needed to have significant stretches when we could just sit and breathe, moments when we weren't thinking about how and why this all happened, and who caused it.

Day 22: Good to have a small routine. Wake up, get kids ready for church, go to church, lunch afterwards, go to cemetery, come home. At least I've got that to look forward to on Sundays. And while it sounds morose to think going to a cemetery is a part of our routine, Caden said, as we were pulling into the cemetery, that his heart feels good when we go to see Mommy. That he feels a sense of peace. Ten years old and he's teaching me things every day. I'm so glad going to visit Leigh's grave isn't something the kids dread.

The rest of my entry for day 54: *A friend, who lost his wife a few months ago, ends his emails with "peace in the midst of our worlds turning upside down." Maybe that's what I need to pray for. Not that my world would turn right side up, rather that I'd have God's peace in this new "upside-down" world.*

The rest of my entry for day 323: *Just as soon as I'm at the height of anger, I'm challenged with the thought of my present life which, though single and difficult, is intact because of my friendship with Jesus. That he is in my bedroom with me and though I miss the interaction with another human, I will always have Christ. So I'm brought from anger to a quiet peace. A lonely peace. I long for the day when it's just peace.*

As stated before, regretfully, I did not forgive the person who killed Leigh Ann for several years. It wasn't as if I was dwelling on his demise. As I mentioned, he, too, had died in the wreck. Though I hadn't truly forgiven him, I honestly didn't dwell on him much after the first year. I was so busy raising three children, working as a teacher, and attending church that I didn't have the time or desire to dwell on whether or not I should forgive someone posthumously. His family was another story.

To this day I have never heard from the young man's family. I honestly don't know why, though I have a possible reason, which

I'll share in a moment. I would like to think that if my son ran into the back of a thirty-five-year-old mother of three young children, killing her instantly, and all the evidence suggested there was 100 percent fault on his side and zero percent fault on her side, I would feel compelled to seek out the family and apologize. Even if he was also killed in the accident, I would find it necessary to let her family know how immensely sorry I was for his callous driving. During those first few months, I was honestly expecting a knock on the door from his family apologizing and asking for my forgiveness. Then I learned more.

Sometime after I had gone back to work, a coworker pulled me aside and told me she knew the family of young man who killed Leigh Ann. I can remember her sharing that information with me and my instant reaction being that of uncaring anger. The reason she was sharing with me wasn't to inform me that she knew the family, but rather to share with me that a year and a half before Leigh Ann was killed, their only other son had died in a car accident. Their only two sons had died in the span of two years.

Please hear me. I want to be compassionate and truthful at the same time. As a parent, I cannot comprehend the depth of maturity it would take to receive news that my son had died, only to hear the same news being told to me about my only other son less than two years later. I can't put into words how sorry I feel for these parents.

And then I'm brought back to March 6, 2010. Reckless driving cost us everything. Can a situation be so bad that one does not reach out and offer condolences? So, for years I made the decision to put forgiveness on hold toward this young man and his family. I know that is not Christlike, and, based on what I'm about to share, it is unbiblical. But I also know some of you are in the same situation. You've experienced injustice, loss, and pain. And you haven't forgiven the offender. In fact, you've done just the opposite. You've sought revenge. You've seethed with anger, and maybe even right now you are dwelling on how wronged you were and the pleasure you'll receive when justice is served. I hear you.

Your anger is sometimes the only leverage you have left in a situation. Anger and seeking revenge are what gets you through the day as you contemplate and concoct how to make the offender's life as miserable as possible. Our anger and refusal to forgive may be akin to coming home from work and enjoying that predinner cocktail. It takes our minds off the mundane checklist of things we still have to do and allows us to dwell on something we'd like to do. It takes the edge off the chaos we've been placed in and, for a few moments, lets us dangerously dream about things we'd never say in church.

Yet if you're pursuing Christ with any degree of desiring to "take up your cross and follow him," the issue of forgiveness will be unavoidable. You may put this on hold for a week, a month, a year, even several years. But it will be laid before you over and over again, and it will need to be addressed because eventually the toll of not addressing it will be too great.

One thing that helped me was to go to God and wrestle with the topic of forgiveness. I needed to dive into the theological deep end for a while and really see what God wanted from me. What is forgiveness? Who should give it? Who should get it? Was God really wanting me to forgive this person and his family? What did that mean? Would we have to become friends? Would that mean I was OK with what happened? Does that mean that he wins and

I lose? If you'll indulge me for a few moments, I'd like to share a few thoughts.

First of all, there is a difference between God's forgiveness of humans (positional/vertical forgiveness) and humans' forgiveness of each other (relational/horizontal forgiveness). Whereas positional/vertical forgiveness is objective and settled, relational/horizontal forgiveness is subjective and fluid. Seemingly every situation has nuances that make giving and receiving forgiveness incredibly challenging. It was very easy for me to justify not forgiving Leigh Ann's killer, and I had no shortage of people who agreed with me. You may be in a similar situation.

So rather than attempting to address every situation of what-ifs, I thought a better tactic would be to share with you a few biblical passages and principles on forgiveness between humans. As you read the passage, may you "wrestle" with God as to how it might apply to your situation.

Passage: "For this reason I say to you, her sins, which are many, have been forgiven, for she loved much; but he who is forgiven little, loves little" (Luke 7:47).
Principle: Truly understanding how much God forgave you produces a heart of love that allows you to greatly forgive others.

Passage: "Bearing with one another, and forgiving each other, whoever has a complaint against anyone; just as the Lord forgave you, so also should you" (Col 3:13).
Principle: Remember Jesus as your model and try to forgive in a similar way.

Passage: "He who conceals a transgression seeks love, but he who repeats a matter separates intimate friends" (Prov 17:9).

Principle: Forgiveness can provide much goodness to your soul.

Passage: "And forgive us our debts, as we also have forgiven our debtors" (Matt. 6:12).

Principle: You have to be willing to grant others forgiveness if you desire to receive God's forgiveness.

Passage: "Be on your guard! If your brother sins, rebuke him; and if he repents, forgive him. And if he sins against you seven times a day, and returns to you seven times, saying, 'I repent,' forgive him" (Luke 17:3-4).

Principle: Forgiving may need to be a recurring conversation with someone. Incredibly difficult for sure but remember your strength will come from experiencing God's never-ending forgiveness toward you.

Passage: "Never take your own revenge, beloved, but leave room for the wrath of God, for it is written, 'Vengeance is Mine, I will repay,' says the Lord" (Rom. 12:19).

Principle: Only God's vengeance brings exact and right justice. Trust in His timing.

And if these principles weren't enough, let me leave you with few more I've heard over the years. While they are not attached to a Bible verse, they seem to make good sense.

Principle: Forgiveness will never be easy, but don't let the difficulty of forgiving be a reason not to forgive.

Principle: If someone seeks your forgiveness, leave it up to God to determine the level of sincerity.

Principle: Forgiveness should never be confused with approving of someone's actions. Forgiveness does not negate the fact that sin is sin.

Principle: Forgiveness may also need to involve boundaries. Toxic relationships can be forgiven but do not have to be maintained.

Connecting with Jesus

"I find no guilt in this man," said Pilate. The night before Jesus's crucifixion, Pilate spoke these words to the chief priests and the multitudes. And he was right. That should have settled the matter. Jesus should have been released. "But they kept on insisting..."

You can imagine as Jesus watched this unfold, how tempting it would have been, in his humanity, to unleash an army of angels upon this ungodly crowd and stop the madness right there. Instead, Jesus was transferred from Pilate to Herod, and he remained silent as the chief priests and scribes spent the night "accusing Him vehemently." Herod and his soldiers, "after treating Him with contempt and mocking Him," sent Jesus back to Pilate, who told the crowds, "I have found no guilt in this man regarding the charges which you make against Him. No, nor has Herod, for he sent Him back to us; and behold, nothing deserving death has been done by Him."

Again, though the false accusations and vehement mocking were completely uncalled for, most people in Jesus's position would be pretty upset but ultimately thankful that at least the person in charge is seeing things the right way. "But they cried out all together, saying 'Away with this man, and release for us Barabbas!'" "Why, what evil has this man done? I have found in Him no guilt demanding death; I will therefore punish Him and release Him." "Crucify, crucify Him!" "And their voices began to prevail."

This account is from the Gospel of Luke 23:4–23. I'm beyond grateful to Luke for including the play-by-play of Jesus's trial for one primary reason: It allows me to better understand the gravity of Luke 23:34. "Father, forgive them; for they do not know what they are doing." Had Luke given a brief summary of what took place the night before Jesus's death, I think we would get to verse 34 and appreciate Jesus extending the proverbial olive branch. But because we have details of how much injustice was done to our Savior, it seems incredible that he actually requested this from God.

"Father, forgive them; for they do not know what they are doing."

Don't forget that Jesus utters these inexplicable words while suffocating on the cross after he endured several hours of being grotesquely tortured by Roman professionals. Additionally, immediately after he asks God to forgive his accusers we read, "And they cast lots, dividing up His garments among themselves." One verse later we find the "rulers were sneering at Him." And after that, "the soldiers also mocked Him, coming up to Him, offering Him sour wine."

I will never understand the strength it took for Jesus to turn his attention to the Father and seek forgiveness on behalf of such an undeserving group of people. But I will forever be grateful for the model Jesus provided.

I will never understand the strength it took for Jesus to turn his attention to the Father and seek forgiveness on behalf of such an undeserving group of people. But I will forever be grateful for the model Jesus provided.

If you're experiencing loss and anger is consuming you, please know I'm not playing judge and jury. I know this is complex and takes time. There are no easy answers. I know what it's like to be alone at two o'clock in the morning, crying tears that no one will see. I know that moment of feeling so overwhelmed when the day hasn't even begun. And I know how good it feels to point to an actual person and to justly feel anger for all the pain they've caused. I understand.

I also know God knows what he's talking about. If we're called to forgive, we can trust God and know his plan is always the best plan. It wasn't easy for me, and I promise it won't be easy for you. But I know what freedom feels like. I want you to be free.

And may Jehovah-Rapha, the God who heals, lead you beside still waters and heal your wounded heart. Ask him for the strength to forgive and experience the blessing of trusting the Lord in most difficult of circumstances.

Chapter Three

Widespread Anger, Part 2

And my soul is greatly horrified; But You, Lord—how long?
—Psalm 6:3

Recently, I was surrounded by three sets of married couples who were enjoying a vibrant discussion on the keys to a good marriage. Each couple was providing experiential wisdom that included the usual advice: Be a good listener; sacrifice for your spouse; laughter is paramount. Everyone was in agreement and everything was making sense until one of the couples proclaimed, "We don't fight."

After a moment of contemplation from the other couples, the need to clarify was evident.

"You mean this past week, right?"

"No, we mean we don't fight. We've been married for over twenty years, and we can't remember the last time we fought."

"You mean you haven't had knock-down, drag-out arguments, right?"

"No, we mean we don't get angry with each other."

"Seriously?"

"Seriously."

I would like to believe that couple. In fact I think I advised them that if that truly was the case, they needed to write a book and begin touring. Instant fame and fortune await them. Who among us would not pay a small fortune to learn and apply principles that would guarantee a relationship void of anger and animosity?

As I left that evening, I couldn't help but wonder one thing: Is being anger-free the benchmark of a great relationship? Certainly, we would agree that anger has the potential to cause great harm and often is the emotion associated with regrettable thoughts and actions. And yet I would be dishonest if I did not disclose that not only was I angry at the young man who killed Leigh Ann, but some of my highest grievances were levied against the God of all creation, and I didn't like that. I knew enough about God and enough about me to understand that it was highly questionable to be angry with the One who not only created me but also saved me. But I couldn't help it. No one was providing sufficient answers as to why this happened, and I knew enough theology to conclude God had those answers. And he wasn't saying much. So, I was angry with him.

Day 5: Dear God, the pain that is beginning to set in is intense. I can't see the goodness. I know you're near to me but I don't want that. I want my wife back. I wanted us to grow old together and then die and experience heaven together. So what happened to the plan? Why would that have been so wrong? What is so appalling to you about me wanting to watch my wife love on our children? Now that you've taken my wife, when's my turn? And how awful would it be if you took me home and left three kids without a mother or father? How easy would it have been for you to change one minute of your plan? One minute and the stoplight wouldn't have been red when she approached. One minute. I guess I didn't know I had to pray for those things. I can't see your goodness. All I see is you taking Leigh Ann from us. You've allowed my wife to die and you've allowed my kids to live without a mother. How wrong is that?

I think I would have been swallowed up in that anger had it not been for the many examples I found when reading through, ironically, the Bible. God's autobiography includes several examples of his creation becoming angry with him. Two in particular that stuck out to me were, again, Job and David.

As I flipped through the Bible hoping to find justification for my anger, I stumbled upon these passages that became the anthem of my indignation.

Is it right for You indeed to oppress, to reject the labor of Your hands, and to look favorably on the schemes of the wicked? (Job 10:3)

But now He has exhausted me; You have laid waste all my company. You have shriveled me up, it has become a witness; and my leanness rises up against me, it testifies to my face. (Job 16:7-8)

Know then that God has wronged me, and has closed His net around me. Behold, I cry, "Violence!" but I get no answer; I shout for help, but there is no justice. He has walled up my way so that I cannot pass, and He has put darkness on my paths. He has stripped my honor from me and removed the crown from my head. He breaks me down on every side, and I am gone; and He has uprooted my hope like a tree. He has also kindled His anger against me and considered me as His enemy. (Job 19:6-11)

How long, O Lord? Will You forget me forever? How long will You hide Your face from me? How long shall I take counsel in my soul, Having sorrow in my heart all the day? How long will my enemy be exalted over me? Consider and answer me, O Lord my God; Enlighten my eyes, or I will sleep the sleep of death. (Ps. 13:1-3).

I will say to God my rock, "Why have You forgotten me? Why do I go mourning because of the oppression of the enemy?" As a shattering of my bones, my adversaries revile me, while they say to me all day long, "Where is your God?" (Ps. 42:9-10)

And the anger of the Lord burned against Uzzah, and God struck him down there for his irreverence; and he died there by the ark of God. David became angry because of the Lord's outburst against Uzzah, and that place is called Perez-uzzah to this day. (2 Sam. 6:7-8)

At the time, I had no concept of the Unwanted Fraternity. I was finding solace with others who understood what it felt like to be completely honest with God—anguished souls who were free to lash out at their Creator, seemingly without penalty. And I realized I wasn't being angry with God as much as I was lamenting.

Day 44: Anger would be a good word to describe my tone. Mondays are usually tough days and after getting through a day of teaching, I wasn't in the mood to get hit with another wave of grief. Just thought I'd let God know I'm not a fan of him allowing Leigh to die when she had so much more life to live. I know God heard my cries, but the van was quiet nonetheless.

Day 63: Mother's Day. We made our way to Leigh's grave and the "dark clouds" had rolled in once again. I wanted to celebrate her life, her being an awesome mother, her being an influence to other moms, but all I could feel was immense sadness that she couldn't be honored today. I felt like she was getting ripped off. I brought three helium balloons with us to the grave. I had markers and told the kids to write a message to Mommy, and after they were done writing, I told them we'd release them up to heaven. Six-year-old Bailey wrote, "Dear Mom, I'm sorry about dying, and Happy Mother's Day." I couldn't agree more. I'm so sorry Leigh had to die, and today the weight of her death seemed especially heavy. "Father, I'm tired and lonely. I don't know why Leigh had to go so soon. It makes me angry. Why couldn't the kids have a mother they could wish a 'Happy Mother's Day' to? She was such a great mom."

Day 136: I'd be lying if I said the sadness has left me. I'd be lying if I said that times like last night leave me confused, frustrated, and, dare I say, angry that Leigh died, that God let her die.

Is it a theological cop-out to suggest I was lamenting rather than being angry with God? Is there a difference? Is one excusable and the other a sin? In describing the genre of the Psalms known as "lament psalms," author and counselor Dan Allender says,

> A person who laments may sound like a grumbler—both vocalize anguish, anger, and confusion. But a lament involves even deeper emotion because a lament is truly asking, seeking, and knocking to comprehend the heart of God. A lament involves the energy to search, not to shut down the quest for truth. It is passion to ask, rather than to rant and rave with already reached conclusions. A lament uses the language of pain, anger, and confusion and moves toward God.[3]

Yes, I was angry at God for allowing Leigh Ann to die. And there were days I didn't want to think about how good may come of this or how this is a part of his plan. But overall, I did desperately want to move closer to God, not push him away. I chose to continue to believe in his character, especially his love for Leigh Ann, me, and the kids. For me, there was a freedom to be honest but never at the expense of denying who I knew my Father to be— sovereign, compassionate, and good. Maybe that's why I was able to pen the following on day 364.

Day 364: This is a day to cry, to mourn, to grieve. I've been doing it since I woke up. But it is also a day to remember Leigh has been in God's presence for a year now. She's in a place many of us are headed, and my guess is she can't wait for us to join her. In the meantime, I'd imagine she would want us to live life well—live by faith, love God and love others, worship our Savior, remember the cross, and enjoy life.

Though we are hurting today may our prayer echo the prophet Habakkuk: "Even though the fig trees have no blossoms, and there are no grapes on the vines; even though the olive crop fails, and the fields lie empty and barren; even though the flocks die in the fields, and the cattle barns are empty. Yet I will rejoice in the Lord! I will be joyful in the God of my salvation! The Sovereign Lord is my strength! He makes me as surefooted as a deer, able to tread upon the heights" (Hab. 3:17–19, NLT).

At some point, in our misery, we have to find that balance between expressing our raw emotions and clinging to what we know to be the truth. Lamenting allowed me to eliminate walls between myself and Abba Father. I was able to live in a secured sense of freedom, knowing that there was nothing I could say to him that would result in diminished love.

> *Lamenting allowed me to eliminate walls between myself and Abba Father. I was able to live in a secured sense of freedom, knowing that there was nothing I could say to him that would result in diminished love.*

How long could I have stayed angry at God? I'm not sure. I do believe God patiently accepted my laments because he knew my heart's desire was to be healed from my pain not through vices or revenge but by the God who heals, Jehovah-Rapha. If you are also lamenting, God hears your cries.

Connecting with Jesus

What a moment it must have been for Peter (then known as Simon) and his brother Andrew to see Jesus along the coastline of the Sea of Galilee and to hear him say to them, "Follow Me." Their reaction says it all: "Immediately they left their nets and followed him." (Mark 1:18). They hadn't a clue as to the three-year adventure they were about to embark on with their Messiah. One wonders if Jesus had given them a preview of what was to come and what was to be expected of them, whether they would have been so eager to follow? Nonetheless, Peter and Andrew, along with the other disciples, got behind their rabbi and followed in his steps.

I'm thankful the Scriptures allow us to see that those three years the disciples spent with Jesus were as authentic a relationship as we'll ever see and serves as a model of how we should view our relationship with God. What a disingenuous story we would read if the disciples simply followed Jesus from town to town, listening to him preach the good news and watching him perform miracles, with no thoughts, emotions, questions, or even disagreements. Rather, the four gospel accounts provide a wealth of examples of genuine relationships being forged between Jesus and the twelve.

> When He got into the boat, His disciples followed Him. And behold, there arose a great storm on the sea, so that the boat was being covered with the waves; but Jesus Himself was asleep. And they came to Him and woke Him, saying, "Save us, Lord; we are perishing!" He said to them, "Why are you afraid, you men of little faith?" (Matt. 8:23-26)

For He was teaching His disciples and telling them, "The Son of Man is to be delivered into the hands of men, and they will kill Him; and when He has been killed, He will rise three days later." But they did not understand this statement, and they were afraid to ask Him. (Mark 9:30-32)

Philip said to Him, "Lord, show us the Father, and it is enough for us." Jesus said to him, "Have I been so long with you, and yet you have not come to know Me, Philip? He who has seen Me has seen the Father." (John 14:8-9)

But Jesus, conscious that His disciples grumbled at this, said to them." (John 6:61)

It would seem fitting if Jesus gave his disciples the pink slip and selected a new group! Time and time again they acted, well, rather humanly. And like a loving friend, Jesus allowed them to express their thoughts and emotions without feeling condemned. He didn't give up on them. Rather, he encouraged them.

Do not let your heart be troubled; believe in God, believe also in Me. In My Father's house are many dwelling places; if it were not so, I would have told you; for I go to prepare a place for you. If I go and prepare a place for you, I will come again and receive you to Myself, that where I am, there you may be also. (John 14:1-3)

In the end, not only did the disciples have a healthy respect for their relationship with Jesus, every one of them (except Judas) would grow in their faith and change the world for Christ.

May we take our cue from the men and women who have figured out that a relationship with God is wholistic. God is deeply interested in every part of our being, including our emotions. He's not threatened in the least when we come to him in our raw states of lament. In fact, it's quite the opposite. Perhaps it is during our most vulnerable times when our relationship with God is in its purest form.

God wants to hear from you. Please don't wait until the tears have dried.

Chapter Four

Earnest Doubting

*Trust in the Lord with all your heart, and do not lean
on your own understanding. In all your ways acknowledge
Him, and He will make your paths straight.*

—Proverbs 3:5

I became a Christian when I was a freshman at Arizona State University. I can recall the day, the prayer, and the dorm room. I remember riding my bike to the campus gym, where one of my friends was practicing dance, and leaving a note on the door outside that read, "I did it!" Since that day, my faith has defined me. My occupations, my academic achievements, the way Leigh Ann and I were raising our children, all had our Christian faith at their nucleus. For over thirty years, my identity has been rolled up into a worldview that includes a right relationship between myself and my Creator. I have enjoyed titles such as reverend, pastor, ordained minister, teacher. People have listened to me, time and time again, give messages that promoted trusting, following, and obeying the Lord. So I knew I was in uncharted waters during that first year when I began to earnestly doubt the very subject I had been promoting my entire adult life.

"*Where are you?*"

This was my last text to Leigh Ann. Somewhat morose considering that when I had asked that question, my wife was no longer alive. Cruel ironies like this came in droves, which naturally led to questioning God as to why all of this was happening. I quickly learned that my new reality was going to be complex—much more complex than the well-intentioned but rather unsubstantial comments the kids and I received in the days that followed, telling us we'll be OK, she's in a better place, or she's an angel looking down on us.

The complexity is derived from these fascinating brains God has given us, brains that are able to spend the days following a dreadful event trying to piece everything together as if we could demonstrate in a courtroom setting that the event shouldn't have occurred, and if that is the case, well then, history would have to be rewritten and our suffering would cease. And so we contemplate, wonder, fixate, and become consumed with the what-ifs until our present day is marked by how many days we made it out of bed and how many days we didn't.

This new reality is also complex because the human experience of grief involves so much more than the initial event. A cascade of new questions at the back of my brain demanded my immediate attention day and night: *What does the future hold for you now? Who are you in light of what has happened? How will you make it on your own? How could God have allowed this to happen?*

I knew these were legitimate questions that needed answers. But I also sensed a defiant freedom I hadn't felt before, a freedom that allowed me to talk to God like I was talking with a friend who had sorely disappointed me. I, a finite being, was openly expressing my displeasure with God, an infinite being. And it felt good. Anger toward God very easily led to my questioning and doubting him. His provision, protection, and goodness were all up for grabs.

Throughout year 1, I came to understand that honest doubting can be a normal experience for a person of faith. I've talked to several Fraternity members who affirm this notion.

> *Throughout year 1, I came to understand that honest doubting can be a normal experience for a person of faith.*

I wish I could recall a pivotal moment during that first year when I met God on the proverbial battlefield to have it out once and for all. A place where I could pinpoint the Jacobesque wrestling match when God showed me why the accident happened and all of my doubting faded away. That never happened. I don't know the exact day, but at some point, I began asking myself, *Will this be a long-term experience? Will the rest of my journey of faith be embedded with this overtone of doubt?*

Some would argue yes. Author Lesley Hazleton argues that faith and doubt go hand in hand. Hazelton said that faith has no easy answers: It's difficult and stubborn, and it involves an ongoing struggle, a continual questioning of what we think we know. She said that faith will always be joined by doubt, and that those who don't doubt aren't really exercising faith.[4]

I certainly agree that faith, by its nature, is difficult and stubborn. But I also think Hazleton, a self-proclaimed agnostic, took a rather humanistic view of this issue, looking at it from the ground up, if you will. If your premise begins with there may or may not be a God and challenges naturally produce doubt, then, yes, it would make sense to advance this kind of thinking. If one's morality, what is good and bad, comes out of experience, and your experience with trials is to doubt the existence or control of a higher power, then faith and doubt would be forever linked.

Perhaps the reason we doubt isn't because we're attempting to seek answers but rather to change minds. My doubting of God allowed me to maintain some control. It allowed me to believe I still had some skin in the game. It fostered this notion that I could discuss the affairs of my life with the God of all creation in such a way that he might not only understand my concerns but also that, ultimately, he might acquiesce, maybe reverse history. Because I knew enough to know if there was someone who could reverse history, it would be God.

Doubt empowered me to go the God of all creation with a plan B or at least raise suspicion on his plan A. And at some point, the exhilaration of doubting God needed to be replaced with a serious decision: Was I going to believe in a God who *is* ultimately in control of all things (some use the term *sovereign*) or a God who is ultimately *not* in control of all things?

Deep down, though at times I doubted God's goodness, I never wanted to doubt his sovereignty. For as much as I wanted to dictate my own circumstances, what I really needed was to trust in a God who, even if he heard my prayers and answered them, was still in control and would continue to do whatever was right in his eyes.

> *For as much as I wanted to dictate my own circumstances, what I really needed was to trust in a God who, even if he heard my prayers and answered them, was still in control and would continue to do whatever was right in his eyes.*

So I arrived at a rather significant crossroads early in my journey of grief. Either I could spend my remaining days continually doubting God's plan, or I could spend my days trusting God's plan. I chose the latter, and here is what I learned. My heavenly Father is always in control and deeply enjoys allowing me to be involved in his plan. I'm reminded of the story Jesus tells his followers of a woman who relentlessly pursued a judge to render a verdict in her favor. Finally the judge gives the woman what she wanted, and Jesus equates this to the way God wants us to pray, with fervor and tenacity all through the day and night. God is moved by our passion and is willing to wrestle with us in our deepest moments of pain.

Here are a few of my prayers to God in that first year.

Day 25: Father, thank you for your Word. How much I'm trying to trust in its truths. How much it is getting me through each day. How much hope I have because of where I know Leigh Ann to be and that I will get to see her again. I would ask for your help in giving me wisdom and strength. Wisdom to make right decisions for my kids. Strength to get out of bed each day and face whatever it is you have for me. Thank you for everyone who has wept with us, who have supported us, who have reached out to us, who have loved on us. I am humbled by the love we've received. Leigh Ann is so missed. Please let me know that she is being taken care of.

Day 133: *Father, thank you for a tremendous weekend with friends and family. Thank you for providing a time for sweet fellowship. As my heart continues to break, may I continue to trust in you. Thank you for never letting go of me. Thank you for taking good care of Leigh Ann. Please let her know I love her so much and I miss her tremendously. I love you.*

Day 144: *Father, thank you for saving Leigh and giving her heaven. I don't understand your timing, but I'll trust in you. I pray one day my mourning will be turned to dancing. For now, I pray for your grace and peace.*

Day 162: *Father, I don't have answers for Caden. I probably never will. I pray you will wrap him in your arms tonight. I pray peace over him now and trust that he'll be safe in your arms. Heal his broken heart.*

Day 171: *Father, I praise you for your never-ending love. Your grace is sufficient for me. I don't like what I'm going through, and I so wish things were like they were six months ago. But they're not and my hope and trust are now fully and completely in you. I pray for your peace, strength, and endurance. May I listen to the Spirit as he continues to teach me. Mold me.*

Day 305: *Father, please take care of my kids. They miss their mother and you have her, so I'm asking you to fill the void. Touch their hearts even tonight. I love you even though I don't understand why all this is happening. I'll continue to trust in you because you are good.*

Day 323: *Father, how deep is your love for us. Thank you for not leaving me even in my darkest hour. May my strength to get up each day and put on a smile be only because of the news I can share with others—that there is hope in the One who saved me. You alone are worthy of my praise.*

I'll never know exactly why God chose to allow Leigh Ann to die. I do know part of that has been watching this plan include using Leigh Ann's death for good. And this isn't unique to me. I've talked to many who have experienced tragedies and have seen some good on the other side. I was greatly encouraged at her funeral to see people's faith grow as a result of hearing about her life. Several children have been named after her, which I take great pride in, knowing that as they grow up and ask why they have their names, she'll be mentioned in that conversation. An international nonprofit, Leigh's Mission (www.leighsmission.com), was created by Leigh Ann's best friend. Leigh was a pediatric nurse, and now thousands of children's blankets are going all over the world. I've had the privilege of walking through tragedies with others simply because I can relate.

Maybe the biggest irony was that my doubting caused my faith to actually grow. My questions drew me into deep, serious conversations with God day after day. My first year of grief was also my richest season of faith. And I am still receiving the residual effects almost ten years later. I've been asked if I would trade all of the good that has happened to have Leigh Ann back. And while I refuse to answer a lose-lose question, I will forever stand and testify to the truth of this famous passage in Romans: "And we know that God causes all things to work together for good to those who love God, to those who are called according to His purpose" (Rom. 8:28).

> *Maybe the biggest irony was that my doubting caused my faith to actually grow.*

Perhaps author Brennan Manning got it just right when talking about his faith. He admitted that he is a bundle of paradoxes, one who believes and doubts, hopes and gets discouraged, loves and hates. Manning claims he often feels like an angel who also has an incredible capacity for beer.[5] I can most definitely relate.

Connecting with Jesus

> *My Father, if it is possible, let this cup pass from Me;*
> *yet not as I will, but as Thou wilt.*
> —Matt. 26:39

Jesus was the master at saying the right thing at the right time. The obvious pushback to that statement is "But Greg, Jesus is God! Everything he says is perfect and perfectly timed!" I agree, but with an asterisk. Jesus was, is, and forever will be the second Godhead of the Trinity. But when Jesus arrived on planet Earth through Mary's womb, he did so without all of his "divine powers and prerogatives as God the Son."[6] Paul tells us this much in Philippians chapter 2: "Have this attitude in yourselves which was also in Christ Jesus, who, although He existed in the form of God, did not regard equality with God a thing to be grasped, but emptied Himself, taking the form of a bond-servant, and being made in the likeness of men" (Phil. 2:5–7). The term *emptied himself* comes from the Greek word *kenosis* and carries with it the idea that for thirty-three years, Jesus willingly embraced all of his humanity, even as God the Son.

This is imperative to understand. When pain and suffering cause doubt, children of God need to know their Savior can relate. Take a look again at the first half of Matthew 26:39 and notice what Jesus asks of the Father. He says, "My Father, if it is possible, let this cup pass from Me." In his humanity, Jesus offers God a plan B, a scenario that doesn't involve a gruesome, torturous execution. A plan that doesn't end with the Son bearing the sins of the world, which, in turn, would also mean bearing the wrath of his Father (Rom. 5:9).

But where we often will sit for far too long, "if it is possible, let this cup pass," Jesus quickly moves to where we ultimately need to be. Take a look again at the rest of Matthew 26:39: "yet not as I will, but as Thou wilt." The Son of Man always knew the greater purpose of his life and death. And while he communicated his deepest and most personal thoughts to his Father, he always wanted God's will to be done. Always. Even though it would mean experiencing unimaginable suffering. Author Max Lucado aptly sums up Jesus's Garden Prayer by saying, "Jesus chose to see His immediate struggle as a necessary part of a greater plan. He viewed the Gethsemane conflict as an important but singular act in the grand manuscript of God's drama."[7]

When Jesus taught the disciples to pray in Matthew 6 (well known as the Lord's Prayer), he knew he would have to model every one of those sixty-seven words, including "Thy will be done." And when handed the ultimate test of doubting God's will versus doing God's will, Jesus did not falter. He masterfully said and did the right thing at the right time.

When our painful circumstances cause doubts to surface, may we frame our conversations with God more like Jesus's night in the Garden: "Thy will be done."

Chapter Five

Beautiful Community

Rejoice with those who rejoice, and weep with those who weep.
—Romans 12:15

When Leigh Ann and I got married, she was getting her nursing degree and I was in the middle of getting my master of divinity degree. Though we were both working, and most of our money was going toward our education, we were able to purchase an 860-square-foot townhouse that we called home. It was tiny, but it was ours.

A few years later, when we were pregnant with our first child, Caden, we sold our townhouse and upgraded to a single-family home. We were in heaven. A bigger place with a huge backyard. We thought we would be in this house for a long time, but within four years another house came on the market that caught our attention. A brand-new neighborhood, a prime lot at the end of a cul-de-sac, and a park right next to the house. We didn't think we would qualify, but within a few weeks we were able to sell our house and move into our dream house. We were still in that house when Leigh Ann was killed. Unbeknownst to us, what made that house the best house we would ever have wasn't the house: It was our community.

Sadly, normalcy today for many, especially in a suburban neighborhood, means a lack of community. Neighbors don't know each other, nobody welcomes the new family who moved in, block parties are sparsely attended, everyone pulls into their garages and immediately shuts the door, and we all live in our block fence–guarded backyards. Times weren't always like this. When I was growing up in the 1970s in upstate New York, there were no block fences. Everyone on the street knew each other. We were in each other's homes for hours. We swam in each other's pools even if no one was home! Doors were left unlocked, meals were often shared, and communal parenting took place up and down the street. Add to this that not many were moving in or out, and what you had was community. I think we took those times for granted.

By God's grace, Leigh Ann and I avoided some of the pitfalls of modern-day suburbia. We had established fruitful relationships with our neighbors, and our kids knew each other. We shared meals, participated in block parties, and played in our front yards. We were also involved in our church. Though it was a large church, we knew our senior pastor by name, were in a small group, and were faithful in attending throughout the week. All of our immediate family and many of our close friends lived only a few miles away.

However, with the circumstances of life, sometimes we take community for granted, maybe even wish it away for a bit of alone time. Whether you're an introvert or an extrovert, a 1w2 or a 7w6 Enneagram type, or an ESTJ or an INFP on the Myers-Briggs

Type Indicator, there is something special about having "me time." I admit to enjoying a cup or two of coffee while sitting in my quiet backyard watching the sunrise. Those moments to rest in solitude, ponder your next move, and enjoy God's creation without interruption are not just enviable but necessary. The Bible says there is a "time to be silent" (Eccles. 3:7). Jesus made solitude an essential part of his ministry (Mark 1:35; Luke 5:16, 6:12) and encouraged his disciples to do the same (Mark 6:31). Being alone with the Lord is good.

And yet, I'm going to contend, being alone for long periods of time isn't good. In fact, it's counterintuitive to who we are and counterproductive to what we're called to do. When God said, "Let Us make man in our image, according to Our likeness" (Gen. 1:26), he was embedding into each human a desire for community. This is because the triune God, in whose image we were made, has never been absent from community. Before there were a billion universes or the space in which those universes could exist, there was the Trinity—Father, Son, Holy Spirit. One God, three persons, living in perfect and complete relationship with each other. Too often we humans make a grave error in believing this holy Trinity needs us. Even if mankind never existed, God the Father, God the Son, and God the Holy Spirit would still be perfectly whole, continuing to have matchless community. When God chose to make man in "Our image," he did so knowing that the pinnacle of his creation would be most satisfied when in community.

So while we all need alone time, we were designed to be in rich community with God and his people. And there will rarely ever be a more important time to be in community than when one is devastated by loss.

> *There will rarely be a more important time to be in community than when one is devastated by loss.*

I can't tell you how vital it was, the night of the accident, not only to have people I could call, but to have people who were able to immediately come to my house and grieve with me. That night, solitude or "me time" would have been a terrible place to be. I needed the community I knew so well to be with me in my loss. After my holy huddle with the kids, I picked up my phone and called my older brother. I'm not sure why I called Scott. I could have easily called my mother or father, Leigh Ann's parents, her brother, her sister, my step-siblings, or any number of our close friends. I could have run to our neighbors' homes. I had several options. I called Scott. His wife, Karen, picked up the phone and immediately knew something was wrong. Through tears and a soft, cracking voice, she heard "Leigh Ann was killed in a car accident a couple of hours ago. I don't know what to do." With that, Scott and Karen took on the morose but needed assignment of calling family and friends with the unspeakable news.

I don't know the exact time but it's safe to say that within thirty minutes, our house was standing room only. I stood on our front porch, greeting people with tears, inviting them into a house where wailing, sobbing, weeping, hugging, silence, and praying were occurring all at the same time. Nobody in particular stood out. Nobody made a memorable speech. Nobody brought the most memorable gift. Nobody was trying to upstage anyone. We were all confused, hurt, sad, and desperate for the pain to stop.

Though much of that dreadful night is a blur, I will never forget one moment in particular. It was when I stood in my kitchen, which gave me a vantage point into the main rooms of the house, and I looked to see dozens of people grieving. They had just lost their mother, their daughter, their sister, their friend, and their neighbor. Though I was in immense pain, I remember silently thanking God that we were all in pain together. No one wanted to be there. No one wanted to think about Leigh Ann not being on earth anymore. That night there was something supernatural about sharing that moment together that, I'm going to assert, was a game-changer for many of us in how we were going to be shaped by this loss. We wept together. We prayed together. We sat in silence together. Not over the phone, not through a text. Not weeks later. But that night, face-to-face. And I'm convinced it made all the difference.

You may read this and believe I had it lucky. That I was fortunate to have experienced that first night with so many family members and friends. And you would be right. In fact, I would argue that an additional benefit from spending that awful night together is what C. S. Lewis proposes in *The Joyful Christian* when he says, "Friendship arises out of mere Companionship when two or more of the companions discover that they have in common some insight which the others do not share and which, till that moment, each believed to be his own unique treasure (or burden)."[8] Everyone drove to the house trying to wrap their minds around this catastrophic news thinking, *No one else knows how devastated I am.* And then they soon realized they weren't in this alone. Bonds of friendship were formed that are still impactful today because of the shared experience of grieving together.

During our most vulnerable times we should not call it luck or good fortune if we have a community that grieves with us. When the notice goes out that a believer has experienced a loss, community should be a given. Sadly for so many, that first night and the subsequent nights that follow are often spent alone. To that end, I believe we need to look to our Jewish friends.

For centuries Jewish people have recognized the loss of a loved one as one of the most vital times to practice healthy community. Jewish people believe so firmly in this that they have created detailed guidelines, including when to go to the house, what to bring, and how to talk with the mourners. Shortly after the funeral (which takes place as soon as possible after the death), the home of the mourners will be filled with the Jewish community. This is referred to as *shiva* or *sitting shiva* and lasts for seven days. The idea is rooted in biblical texts including Genesis and Job, where Joseph and Job mourned for seven days (*shiva* meaning "seven" in Hebrew). During shiva, mourners spend a week wearing torn clothing (or a torn black ribbon), they sit low to the ground on stools or on the floor, they do not go to work, nor do they bathe or shave. They refrain from pleasurable activities, which may include studying the Torah. The idea is to take the time to simply stop and mourn. The problem is that the world doesn't stop turning because people are taking time to mourn. This is where the Jewish community shows up in a powerful way. Friends and neighbors spend those seven days with mourners, crying with them, listening to them, and grieving with them. The community also provides menial yet necessary tasks like grocery shopping, paying bills, and doing housework. While I believe too many rules blur the line of authenticity, I wholly admire the Jewish perspective on community care. Christians would be well served to follow suit.

When I look back on my journal entries, I can see shiva being practiced without us even knowing. It began that very first night and continued on throughout the entire week.

Day 3: I believe I "felt" the prayers of the righteous tonight. Thousands have been praying for us, in particular the students at the high school who gathered for a prayer vigil this evening. And I've felt the best I've felt since the news. Still deep, deep in the woods but just a glimmer of feeling better. So many have stopped by and have encouraged me with their words that they and several others are in prayer for me, the kids, and everyone involved. So many people are stopping by to grieve with us. She touched the lives of so, so many. I still can't believe that people won't get the opportunity on earth to meet her. That is truly their loss. But for those of us who knew her, we should count ourselves as blessed. God has been good to us and especially to me. I'll spend the rest of my life trying to figure out why she had to go so soon. But I'll forever be grateful to God for allowing me to be Leigh Ann's husband. She deserved much better, and I couldn't have done any better. I love you so much, Leigh.

Day 4: Leigh, we've all been together for the past three days, and we're hanging in there. Little moments here and there but overall, it's running OK. I'm so tired of hugging people! I know it helps them as much as it helps me. Dr. Shousha came by. It was so nice because he and his wife are so sincere. Knowing how much support I've gotten—I really, really wish this were me that had died. Now I know you would have been taken care of because I'm being taken care of.

Day 5: *Needless to say, hundreds of people were at your viewing. I hugged people for over three hours. People are so loved by you and wanted to let me know that. Some were saying it took them an hour to get inside the building. The line went down the street. Honey, people loved you! I love the fact that I was your husband. I so wish I had more time to tell you how much I love you. I will be lonely beyond words without you.*

Day 7: *My mother, father, brother, Karen, cousin Laurie, Aunt Lynn, cousin Larissa, Ryan, Megan, and others just left. Now it's shower and over to Larry and Peggy's to sit around, eat, and pass the time. Julie and Eric, Andra and Jeremy, and Jarrod and Sara are supposed to come as well. Then I'm taking the kids to church. That actually turned into my brother, Karen, their kids, Dad, Gloria, cousin Laurie, Aunt Lynn, Mom, and her friend Marci also coming.*

And then it continued day after day, week after week. My mentor and friend Kurt Richardson, who lives in Massachusetts, came as quickly as he could after he got the call that Leigh Ann was killed. I can remember meeting him in my front yard and not doing anything but weeping. Two grown men, friends for twenty years, embracing and crying. This would happen over and over. There would be times when so many would reach out, I would hide in my bedroom to avoid more community! What a good problem to have. Shiva really never stopped throughout that first year. Day 26 captures it well.

Day 26: *The support continues. The cards/emails I get from so many telling me that Leigh Ann/this situation is on their minds which leads them to pray. The memorial fund is being added to daily. People continue to bring us meals. Today a lovely woman from our church brought over a meal and three Easter baskets. Are you kidding me? I'd say I'm shocked, but it's been like that in so many situations. People have been led by God to go out of their way to show me/the kids God's love. It's been amazing to watch and be a part of. There's a part of my heart that is bleeding out, and there's another part that is full of joy. Part of that joy has come from the many ways people have expressed their love these past four weeks. It continues to be this profound love, not the Hallmark card kind of love. But this deep, deep community-type love. Amazing, amazing stuff.*

If you are beginning your journey of grief, please reach out to those around you. Risk being vulnerable with neighbors, coworkers, and friends. Allow family members to love on you. Be proactive in calling your church and telling your pastor you are in pain. I beg you to break free from "block-fence living" and allow others to sit shiva with you. You need to mourn, and you need to mourn well. Let the body of Christ help.

As well, be ready to sit shiva with someone else. Recently I received a phone call from a friend who had just been initiated into the Unwanted Fraternity. Marty called me and five others, asking if we would join him and his wife, Cyndee, for an evening around their fire pit. Marty and Cyndee hadn't lost a loved one. Rather, three weeks prior to the invitation, Marty received the terrible news that he had cancer, which had migrated to his brain. Doctors scheduled immediate surgery, and while they were able to successfully remove the two cancerous lesions, Marty was informed that he is far from being completely healed. The doctors must now find the part of Marty's body that is housing the genesis cancer cells and destroy them, hopefully before more cancer spreads throughout his body. Marty and his wonderful wife love Jesus deeply, but this experience caused Marty to raise some profound worldview questions. Though we were not sitting shiva (no one had passed away), we all knew what our role was that evening. Sit. Listen. Pray. Three hours passed, the fire burned down to embers, and then it was time to go. We laughed and cried with Marty and Cyndee, we gave our thoughts only when asked, and then we prayed and sang the doxology. It was Christian community in its purest form.

If you are near to someone who is mourning, please don't miss the opportunity to "weep with those who weep." This is the stunning picture of the body of Christ in action. It's what the apostle Paul proclaims in 1 Corinthians: "And if one member suffers, all the members suffer with it; if one member is honored, all the members rejoice with it. Now you are Christ's body, and individually members of it" (12:26–27). Community is God's way of tangibly taking care of us while we walk this earth. Whether you are just starting this journey or midway through it, your community is a vital part.

I understand the potential for awkward moments. I understand the risk of saying something that will come out the wrong way. I understand the uneasiness of walking into a room and being unsure of how to feel. But I also understand, and have experienced, the supernatural power of healing when the body of Christ comes together in times of sorrow. My anguished soul was comforted by the prayers and encounters with fellow mourners. Grieving is agonizing, but there is much solace when it can be done together.

> *My anguished soul was comforted by the prayers and encounters with fellow mourners. Grieving is agonizing, but there is much solace when it can be done together.*

Connecting with Jesus

As mentioned in the previous chapter, while on earth (according to Philippians chapter 2), Jesus voluntarily relinquished some of the qualities that are rightly his in order to fully embrace his humanity. I like how John Piper says it: "aspects of His glory He laid aside."[9] Much has been written about the "aspects" that are being imagined in this passage. But one aspect Jesus never set aside was his community with God the Father and God the Spirit. Perhaps this is due to the very fact that the Father, Son, and Holy Spirit are all the same, and only, God.

While this book does not have complex theology as its primary aim, to speak of Jesus and community is to primarily speak of the Trinity, which then needs to be defined. The Bible confirms the Trinity as one God (Deut. 6:4) who has a triune nature which consists of the Father, the Son, and the Holy Spirit (John 10:30; Rom. 1:20). Each member of the Godhead is shown to have the same qualities of deity (Isa. 40:13; Matt.11:27; John 2:24), and all parts of the Trinity are coeternal and coequal (Gen. 1:26, 11:7; 2 Cor. 13:14). Finally, and possibly the most profound aspect of the description, there is a complete dependence upon each other with no need for any outside influences (John 8:18, 12:49–50). In other words, God is never in need of any other community outside of complete union between the Father, Son, and Holy Spirit.

Take a moment to let that manifest itself. Before there were any created beings, the Trinity was completely satisfied in community. And since the creation there hasn't been anything created that would be a value-add to the Trinity. Nothing.

But in an act of pure love, God has invited you and me to be a part of his community. In fact, all three persons of the Trinity are active in that invitation.

"Come now, and let us reason together," says the Lord, "Though your sins are as scarlet, they will be as white as snow; though they are red like crimson, they will be like wool." (Isa. 1:18)

Jesus said to them, "I am the bread of life; he who comes to Me will not hunger, and he who believes in Me will never thirst." (John 6:35)

The Spirit and the bride say, "Come." And let the one who hears say, "Come." And let the one who is thirsty come; let the one who wishes take the water of life without cost." (Rev. 22:17)

This select group has thrown open the gates to their perfect community and are inviting their creation to join in! God the Father, the Abba, who loves you unconditionally, wants you to experience community with him, the Son, and the Spirit. Jesus Christ, the Savior, who died for your sins, wants you to experience community with him, the Spirit, and the Father. Holy Spirit, the teacher, who reveals truth to you, wants you to experience community with him, the Father, and the Son. And in doing so, we begin to understand what it's like to live in community with one another.

My heart for you is to live in "beautiful community." If you are not part of a supportive community, I encourage you to look for one. Community is important because it allows others to shoulder some of your burden. And when that is done well, you start to find strength again. This then opens the opportunity for you to be someone else's community. Beautiful community is necessary for those in pain, and they are waiting, even right now, for their doorbell to ring. Let's not disappoint.

Chapter Six

Acutely Alone

Turn to me and be gracious to me,
For I am lonely and afflicted.
—Psalm 25:16

After reading a chapter called "Beautiful Community," it may seem contradictory to read a chapter titled "Acutely Alone." I've been welcoming you into the Unwanted Fraternity and now I'm about to abandon you. It doesn't seem to add up. But I'd be willing to wager that if you've experienced loss, even if this is your day 5, you know even the best moments of community are simply that—moments.

Those moments of community are critical to a healthy journey through one's first year of grief, and one can never get enough of them, especially moments with Fraternity members. But even in the best moments of community, you will undoubtedly, at times, feel deeply alone (this is part of the internal chaos to which Jerry Sittser referred; see chapter 1).

Perhaps this is due to two factors: (1) no one is fully walking in your shoes, and (2) there is an aspect of being alone that can only be remedied by God.

When Leigh Ann was killed, news spread from my house to my brother's house to the houses of every known relative and close friend. An immediate surge of loss swiftly moved throughout the community, and pain began piercing the hearts of hundreds. As previously recalled, what made those first weeks bearable was that nearly everyone I came in contact with was hurting. This made our little community unadulterated, free from niceties and casual talk. We got down to the business of grieving in each other's presence. We all needed that because in that horrifying moment on March 6, 2010, people lost a mother, a daughter, a sister, an aunt, a niece, a granddaughter, a close friend, and a coworker. And I could easily add the words "faithful," "loving," "committed," and "joyful" to those titles, which only accentuated the enormity of our loss.

But no one lost Leigh Ann as their wife except me.

No one will ever know Leigh Ann as their helpmate except me. No one except me will ever know the feeling of standing across from this beautiful woman in 1996 as she said "I do," beaming because she chose me. No one got to experience the depth of Leigh Ann's joys and heartaches like I did. And no one had a closer seat than I did to witness what agape love looked like between a mother and her children. There are things my beautiful community just couldn't understand (though they desperately tried to), and, therefore, they couldn't help me.

I'm not unique. The painful reality for those who loved Leigh Ann was realizing there will always be a part of this journey that must be walked alone. I saw this firsthand with my kids. I have tried to help them as best I know how, but I will never know what it's like to instantly lose my mother as a ten-year-old. Nor will I ever know what it's like to go to my mother's grave at six years of age and write on a Mother's Day balloon, "Dear Mom, I'm sorry about dying, and Happy Mother's Day." And I'll never know what it's like to mostly remember my mother through pictures and videos because she died when I was four years old.

I will be forever grateful for the unwavering community the kids and I had in year 1 (and continue to have now). But my journal also reminds me of the many days I felt truly alone as I walked through that first year as a widower and single father.

Day 26: It wasn't supposed to be like this. I shouldn't have to hear Bailey pray that he was so glad his school didn't burn down in the fire drill he had and then end his prayer with letting God know that he misses his mom "so much." It's not supposed to be the case where Caden has to ask his grandmother to sleep over because he's just not used to having only one adult in the house.

So many times today I've wanted to text, call, or talk to Leigh Ann. Things only she'd understand. Things that I now have to bottle up. I can journal or tell someone else, but it's not the same.

Day 63: After work I went to the cemetery to wish Leigh a happy anniversary. Cried hard. Just didn't seem real that I was spending my anniversary at the cemetery. Crying makes you tired, and maybe that's why this evening I feel exhausted. Been crying a lot.

After putting the kids to bed Saturday, I was reminded by how tired I was that this (single parenting) is my new reality. This isn't a test to see if I'd make a good parent. No one is going to knock on the door and tell me it's over. Raising three kids, even with all the help (and I have tons of help), is exhausting. Always something to do, someone in need of something. And it's less than exciting to think tomorrow will be more of the same. More baths to give, more backs to scratch, more shoes to tie, more toys to pick up, more telling the kids to be nice to each other, more trying to find lost things, more times to say "What?" every time someone says "Dad?" And no more of being able to tell Leigh things that I'm going through. Little things, work things, friend things, family things, kid things. No things. It's that combination of extremely busy with life and no spouse to share this busy life with that often feels like a one-two knockout punch. Maybe the prayers of the saints and God's goodness is what helps me get up off the canvas each day, because for some reason I keep getting up.

Day 73: *I thought coming off of a difficult weekend a couple weeks ago I'd see some better days. And maybe just getting through each day means progress is being made. But it feels like I'm losing the battle.*

Leigh's been gone for over seventy days now. My memory often fails me and I can't remember all the specifics. Sometimes I can remember what her laugh sounded like and sometimes I can't. Sometimes I can remember what she looked like in a certain outfit and sometimes I can't. Sometimes I can remember her smile and sometimes I can't.

I woke up this morning and I can barely remember what it's like to wake up with someone else in your bedroom. What it's like to brush your teeth with someone else brushing their teeth. What it's like to have a conversation with someone while getting dressed. Basically, what it's like to be married. I'm amazed at how quickly I'm forgetting these things. Being married, as most know, is hard work. One of the perks, though, is getting to live your life with someone, especially someone you love. So going from being with Leigh 24/7 to being totally deprived of seeing her, hearing her, smelling her, and holding her continues to wreak havoc on my life, starting from the moment I wake up.

For those who are wanting a few prayers to fix the situation or make me feel better, this journey may not be the one for them. I am counting on some better days in the years to come, but for now it is still more of the same. Constantly thinking, constantly tired, a few bright moments each day but constantly in mental and emotional anguish. I'm sorry this isn't working out the way our culture thinks it should. Quick, easy, neat. Say a few prayers, let enough time pass, cry a little, and then move on. Believe me, I wish it would be that formulaic. I'm very, very tired of "more of the same."

Day 96: *The new schedule has shown me with great clarity that I am in fact single. To be more specific, I'm a single father. I have plenty of help, for which I'm grateful. But all the help in the world doesn't keep me from thinking and acting like a father who is parenting without the help of a mother. The kids have become my life. I think about them constantly—where they are, what they're doing, what they're thinking. I can ask for advice* *from others, but I'm the final decision maker when it comes to Caden, Bailey, and Malia. From deciding what to wear, what to eat, what to do, what advice to give, who to spend time with, what discipline to administer, how to handle a sibling fight, when to put them to bed, and what to spend money on. Those are a few of the decisions. Then there are the dozens of parental "acts" that take place each day. I realized this week that the "new reality" has just begun. It's not a matter of placing events on the calendar so we have things to look forward to. My reality is waking up each day as my kids' only parent and trying my best to "train them up in the ways of the Lord." It's more difficult than I could have ever imagined.*

Honestly, I despise this "new reality." I despise feeling single and alone.

Day 124: *"Who stole the cookies from the cookie jar? Malia stole the cookies from the cookie jar." Malia came into my room tonight and asked if she could have a cookie. I specifically told her she could have one cookie before bed. Bailey followed Malia by fifteen minutes asking if he could have five cookies. "No, you may have one cookie." "Then why does Malia get five?" After summoning Malia to my room, she entered with three cookies in her hand, and chocolate all over her cheeks. There were questions asked, justifications given, and lots of darting eyes. Malia did hear me say only one cookie and she disobeyed me and took five. It's two minutes to bedtime. What do I do?*

I sent Malia to her room and told her I'd be in to discuss her poor choices. When I walked in, she was lying on her bed, blankets over her face. I was at a loss for words knowing that she was ready to lose it at any moment. "Malia, I need you to know that taking five cookies makes Daddy feel bad, because I told you to take only one. Now when you ask me for a cookie, I'll have to come with you to make sure you only take one. Do you understand?" The loud sobbing began. It's late, I'm tired, and now I feel bad that my daughter is crying her little eyes out because she thinks she's done something terrible.

I laid down next to her and put my arm around her and let her cry until she was done. I wanted to communicate to her that I will always love her even when things don't go so well. Maybe by just being there, snuggled together, she got the message. The crying eventually stopped and we lay there until she told me she was OK. At least one of us was OK. I can't tell you how much I missed Leigh Ann in that very moment.

Day 244: *Dear Leigh Ann,*

I have to hope that your night is going better than mine. Caden and Bailey are crying themselves to sleep for missing you so much. Caden has put up such a good fight these past few months, but tonight he was tired of fighting. "I know Mommy is in heaven, but I get so impatient and I want to see her again so badly." I cried with him, trying to encourage him that we may have to wait another fifty years, but there will come a day when Mommy will never not be there. We both cannot wait to see you again.

As I walked into Bailey's room, I found him crying, holding a picture of the both of you. You meant the world to both him and Caden, and though I don't think I could stand to see everyone crying night after night, it was good for us to admit we don't have this new life figured out yet.

Malia was bouncing from room to room trying to make the boys laugh. She hates when we're all sad.

I reaffirmed to Caden tonight that it just isn't fair that you were taken so early in life. He said, "Mom must be so special to God, because he took her to such a great place at such a young age." I know he's right, but I wanted to cry out, "That doesn't make it any easier on us though. What about all she's missing and all we're missing and how hard living has become? When is God going to make sense of all of this? Who wants to live another moment without Mom?" Instead I just cried a little more with him.

I love you, Leigh Ann. I love everything about you, and I want to tell you that over and over and over again. Regardless of you being my wife, I just think you are a woman worth knowing. You simply don't know how many times I've said or have heard others say, "I wish Leigh were here, she'd know what to do..."

Eight months into this and I can't say I'm any further along. I don't feel like I am anyway. I'm trying hard to live with hope, but some days it just seems like our reunion is so far away.

I love you so much,
Me

A newly introduced Fraternity member, whom I met early in my "new reality" of being a widower and single father, gave me great insight into being alone. I shared with him that I was often alone but didn't necessarily want to be around others. Prior to Leigh's death, I enjoyed company, but I was also content in spending time by myself (am I the only one who enjoys an occasional solo trip to the movies?!). What I was challenged with, I mentioned, was the feeling of loneliness whether I'm around people or by myself. My friend described it as being more metaphysical, a constant feeling of isolation if you will. It's like living in a state of being separated from that one meaningful relationship. For me that relationship would be with my wife. For others it may be a child or a parent. It's not that I don't have other meaningful relationships; I just don't have one with the most meaningful person to me. The one I could share every part of my life with. The one I could be romantic with. The one I could dream big dreams with. The one I could be myself with. The one I've been used to for so many years. The one I associated with this pretty blond-haired, awesome woman, who was smart, beautiful, and amazing in a thousand different ways. The one I knew as Leigh Ann, my wife, my love.

> *It's not that I don't have other meaningful relationships; I just don't have one with the most meaningful person to me.*

After that conversation, I knew my acute aloneness was an aspect of my journey that could only be remedied by God.

I try hard not to provide simplistic answers to deeply formed questions. When someone asks me a question I know matters greatly to them, I want to honor them with a thoughtful and meaningful response. Notwithstanding, if you are struggling in your aloneness, the most thoughtful response I have for you is admittedly simple: Spend time with the Lord.

When diagnosing loneliness, psychologists and behaviorists sometimes use terms such as "alone-together" and "alone-alone" to better understand and treat a patient.[10] The terms describe two scenarios that could occur during early infancy. When a child has gained complete trust in their parents, the parents are able to physically distance themselves for brief periods of time and the child, though alone, will still feel together (alone-together). However, if the parents prolong being absent, the child can lose trust and feel abandoned (alone-alone), which, over time, could result in isolation and aloneness due to a lack of trust.

Though you may be alone right now in your journey, don't ever forget you are "alone-together" with God. He may feel distant to you, but nothing has changed about your relationship with him. Unlike the parent who may occasionally leave the child, your Father will never leave you. He's in the very space you're in right now! You can continue to trust the Lord as much as you did prior to your loss, if not more. This is what the Scriptures declare, so read them, friend, and let God's Word declare to you, you are not alone!

> *You can continue to trust the Lord as much as you did prior to your loss, if not more. This is what the Scriptures declare, so read them, friend, and let God's Word declare to you, you are not alone!*

"Do not fear, for I am with you; do not anxiously look about you, for I am your God. I will strengthen you, surely I will help you, surely I will uphold you with My righteous right hand" (Isa. 41:10).

For my father and my mother have forsaken me, but the Lord will take me up. (Ps. 27:10)

Why are you in despair, O my soul? And why have you become disturbed within me? Hope in God, for I shall yet praise Him, The help of my countenance and my God. (Ps. 42:11)

Be anxious for nothing, but in everything by prayer and supplication with thanksgiving let your requests be made known to God. And the peace of God, which surpasses all comprehension, will guard your hearts and your minds in Christ Jesus. (Phil. 4:6-7)

Being acutely alone and trusting in the Lord for your aloneness will often run in tandem. Meaning, it's far too simple to suggest reading these verses will fill a void of loneliness. But this much I know, for as much as my journal is peppered with entries declaring loneliness, there are as many asking God to fulfill his promises. I asked that not only for myself but also for those closest to me, for I knew only God can truly heal the broken and lonely heart.

Day 151: Dentist visit and "Meet the Teacher" night. In both situations Leigh Ann would have been the "go-to" parent. She would have been the kids' first choice for comfort, wisdom, encouragement. I don't say this for any other reason than it's true. Leigh Ann would have known what to say to Caden when she saw a tear roll down his eye as he tried his best to maintain a stiff upper lip at the dentist. Instead, he had his goofball dad taking pictures. Leigh would have known what questions to ask the teachers tonight.

Looking down the road at the countless times each of our kids will need a "mother's touch," only to find their dad staring back at them, forces me to a place I've never been before. A place of wholly trusting God to provide for my kids. No one else can fill the void Leigh has left. God has to do that for Caden, Bailey, and Malia. He has to show them he's in control and he will provide for them. That life will be not only OK but actually good. And that though they will be without a mother, they are never without their Father. I'm taking Jesus at his word when he says, "I will never leave you nor forsake you" (Heb. 13:5). God deserves my praise no matter my circumstances, but how much more I want to praise him knowing he's going to take care of my kids in the areas I simply cannot.

As I write this chapter, our world is experiencing a pandemic with COVID-19. Tens of thousands have died from this virus, and because as of today there is no vaccine, the protocol for anyone who tests positive is fourteen days of self-isolation and a hospital stay if symptoms worsen. This new way of living became very real for us when Caden, now twenty years old, tested positive for the virus. Upon discovering that his girlfriend had tested positive, Caden got tested and immediately began self-isolation. Though his symptoms were mild compared to others', Caden adhered to being isolated and thus didn't feel physical touch from anyone for over a week. All his meals and drinks were left at his bedroom door. He used a separate bathroom. We talked to him from several feet away, and the entire family knew under no circumstances were they to be in physical contact with their brother. Caden and I have compared notes on his experience and my first year of being a widower. I was saddened that there were even a few similarities.

But, more than once, I walked by Caden's room and saw him reading his Bible and studying God's Word. It's then that I'm encouraged, because I remember that, though this is his journey, he's not alone.

Connecting with Jesus

Jesus and I do not have much in common, but one thing we share (as do many of you) is knowing what it's like to have beautiful community and at the same time experience being alone.

For Jesus, aloneness came in two forms: rejection and choice.

Jesus's aloneness wasn't always visible, nor was it just a time to recharge. Jesus had a wildly popular ministry for three years, but it also came with a healthy dose of rejection. In fact, Isaiah prophesied about this, proclaiming Jesus was going to be "despised and forsaken of men" (Isa. 53:3). The Gospels give us glimpses of these moments of rejection. When Jesus was preaching in his hometown of Nazareth, "they took offense at Him" (Matt. 13:57). When he was attempting to enter a village of Samaritans, "they did not receive Him" (Luke 9:53). He told his own disciples, "But first He must suffer many things and be rejected by this generation" (Luke 17:25), and "You will all fall away because of Me this night, for it is written, 'I will strike down the shepherd, and the sheep of the flock shall be scattered'" (Matt. 26:31). Even after Jesus comes back to rule and reign on earth, he will face rejection (Rev. 20:7–8). Jesus knows what it feels like to be alone due to rejection.

There are also several passages in the Gospels that indicate Jesus willingly spent time alone. Before Jesus began preaching in Galilee, "He arose and went out and departed to a lonely place (Mark 1:35). Before he chose the twelve disciples, he "went off to the mountain" with no one else (Luke 6:12). After feeding the five thousand, Jesus sent the crowd away and "went up to the mountain by Himself" (Matt. 14:23). Luke records that Jesus "would often slip away to the wilderness" (Luke 5:16). We don't know all of the reasons why Jesus chose certain times to be in solitude, but we do know what he did when he was alone. One thing. Jesus prayed. Every passage listed above specifically mentions Jesus praying when he was alone.

What Jesus prayed for is between him and the Father. But I have to imagine Jesus's prayers weren't that different from yours or mine. Why? Because Jesus was experiencing life. He was experiencing rejection, loss, and pain. He was experiencing the pressure of making decisions that would impact the whole of humanity. He was experiencing all of the emotional highs and lows of ministering to people. So Jesus did what so many of us fail to do. He chose God over man. He chose to fellowship, commune, and be with the One who could perfectly love, comfort, strengthen, and empower. Jesus put a premium on staying connected to God the Father through countless hours of solitude and prayer.

Regardless of why you're alone right now, my encouragement is to take advantage of this time. I can only say "I get it," because I do. The horrific reality of sleeping alone, eating alone, cleaning the house alone, watching a movie alone, going to church alone, and crying alone is one a person should not have to experience. But, for whatever reason, you find yourself in that very situation. Please consider spending more time with the Lord, not less. Please consider establishing daily encounters with the Lord through prayer and worship. Please consider following Jesus's model and being proactive in seeking out solitude for the purpose of prayer.

If you begin a habit of continual fellowship with God through prayer during your darkest days, that habit will continue even when you find yourself in a season of rest, for good habits will be hard to break.

Without making promises, I want to assure you the acute loneliness you're experiencing will diminish. Time will get in the way, and slowly, your schedule will begin to fill again. It will feel different for sure. And it will be with different people. But it will be full once again. If you begin a habit of continual fellowship with God through prayer during your darkest days, that habit will continue even when you find yourself in a season of rest, for good habits will be hard to break.

Chapter Seven

Heavenly Hope

In My Father's house are many rooms; if that were not so,
I would have told you, because I am going there
to prepare a place for you.
—John 14:2

P rior to losing Leigh Ann, I really didn't think heavily upon the details of heaven. I just knew that someday I would end up there. Yet after I was told the news of Leigh Ann's death, this question, and every other question I had about the afterlife, took on major significance. I was both impressed and disappointed at how many questions I had about heaven. I couldn't believe how often I thought about what lies ahead for a Christian, which brought me great joy. But I also realized that among all these questions, few had answers. Leigh Ann was a faithful believer in Jesus Christ, so I knew her destination was secured (John 1:12). I knew Jesus was there (John 14:2), as were the saints of old (Rev. 5:11). I knew there was no sorrow or pain (Rev. 21:4) and that Leigh Ann's once broken body was going to be restored and glorified (1 Cor. 15:42).

But I was growing steadily unsatisfied as the number of questions began to outweigh the number of answers. Even one year after Leigh Ann's death, I was perplexed.

> **Day 365:** *I need more facts about heaven than the Bible provides. Did Leigh Ann know what we did yesterday? Did she care? What will love be like between us? How will she relate to the kids? Of course, this leads me to think macro thoughts about heaven, including: How much free will do we possess in heaven? How will what I experience on earth affect me in heaven? If I can't sin in heaven, how will I experience joy, for on this side of heaven often joy is a result of suffering?*

These are not the merely distracting questions my students will sometimes ask to get me off topic. Rather, these are deeply profound, because the answers to these questions (and dozens of others) are what now, in part, determine my true hope of heaven. Ever since March 6, 2010, I have labored over questions that others find nonsensical or not worth their time. Interestingly, when I'm talking with a Fraternity member about the afterlife, there is a nod of the head as if to say, "Please keep talking because I was asking the same questions and all my non-Fraternity family and friends think I'm crazy."

I'm reminded of the famous comedian Jeff Foxworthy and his classic "You know you're a redneck if…" routine. You know you're an Unwanted Fraternity member if you've ever asked the following questions:

If my loved one in heaven is watching me, does she look away when I sin?

I know there isn't sex in heaven, but if it's going to be a few decades until I pass away and see my spouse again, can we make out for just a few minutes when I get there?

Is my loved one in heaven going to forget me because it's been so long since we've seen each other?

Will my family all live in the same heavenly house, and if so, does that include in-laws?

Will my child who passed away grow up in heaven?

Does my loved one in heaven even miss me?

When there aren't concrete answers (especially when asking questions about a place we've never been), we're invited to fill in the blanks with whatever best fits our narrative. Thus myths about heaven are given birth and, once alive, are hard to put to death. The following are just a few.

Myth: Heaven is going to be great because it's all about me.

There's a popular song played in churches today that includes the following lyrics: "You didn't want heaven without us, so Jesus, You brought heaven down."[11] While I believe the author's intentions were pure, that lyric seemingly places the emphasis on mankind, saying that we are one of the main attractions in heaven.

People who view themselves as the most valuable and important feature in existence would possess what is known as an anthropocentric worldview. Life is about you, and therefore your decisions must ultimately benefit you the most. But why stop at life on earth? Why not make the afterlife about you as well? Perhaps this can best be seen on the gravestones of millions whose epitaphs speak of heaven simply being the next place to continue our leisurely activities with the same group of friends. Once everyone passes, we'll all meet up on the first tee box and continue right where we left off. It doesn't matter if you're religious. In fact it might help if you weren't. The last thing we want in heaven are those fundamental Christians!

In this way of thinking, heaven needs to be a place to eat, drink, and be merry. Period. Sure, there can be some cloud surfing and halo-wearing. But for the most part, heaven needs to be an eternity of self-indulgence, much like the animated film *Wall-E*. Pixar brought to life what many envision heaven to be like: relaxing on moving recliners all day and enjoying food, drink, shopping, movies, and gaming without lifting a finger. It doesn't matter if you become pathetically self-indulgent and lethargic. That's what you're supposed to do on your eternal vacation.

Yet in Revelation chapter 4 and part of chapter 5, the apostle John brings to life a starkly different picture of where our focus will be in heaven. Or more fittingly, who will be our focus in heaven.

> After these things I looked, and behold, a door standing open in heaven, and the first voice which I had heard, like the sound of a trumpet speaking with me, said, "Come up here, and I will show you what must take place after these things." Immediately I was in the Spirit; and behold, a throne was standing in heaven, and someone was sitting on the throne. And He who was sitting was like a jasper stone and a sardius in appearance; and there was a rainbow around the throne, like an emerald in appearance. Around the throne

were twenty-four thrones; and upon the thrones I saw twenty-four elders sitting, clothed in white garments, and golden crowns on their heads. Out from the throne came flashes of lightning and sounds and peals of thunder. And there were seven lamps of fire burning before the throne, which are the seven spirits of God; and before the throne there was something like a sea of glass, like crystal; and in the center and around the throne, four living creatures full of eyes in front and behind. The first living creature was like a lion, the second creature like a calf, the third creature had a face like that of a man, and the fourth creature was like a flying eagle. And the four living creatures, each one of them having six wings, are full of eyes around and within; and day and night they do not cease to say, "Holy, holy, holy is the Lord God, the Almighty, who was and who is and who is to come." And when the living creatures give glory, honor, and thanks to Him who sits on the throne, to Him who lives forever and ever, the twenty-four elders will fall down before Him who sits on the throne, and they will worship Him who lives forever and ever, and will cast their crowns before the throne, saying, "Worthy are You, our Lord and our God, to receive glory and honor and power; for You created all things, and because of Your will they existed, and were created." (Rev. 4)

When He had taken the scroll, the four living creatures and the twenty-four elders fell down before the Lamb, each one holding a harp and golden bowls full of incense, which are the prayers of the saints. And they sang a new song, saying, "Worthy are You to take the scroll and to break its seals; for

You were slaughtered, and You purchased people for God with Your blood from every tribe, language, people, and nation. You have made them into a kingdom and priests to our God, and they will reign upon the earth." Then I looked, and I heard the voices of many angels around the throne and the living creatures and the elders; and the number of them was myriads of myriads, and thousands of thousands, saying with a loud voice, "Worthy is the Lamb that was slaughtered to receive power, wealth, wisdom, might, honor, glory, and blessing." And I heard every created thing which is in heaven, or on the earth, or under the earth, or on the sea, and all the things in them, saying, "To Him who sits on the throne and to the Lamb be the blessing, the honor, the glory, and the dominion forever and ever." And the four living creatures were saying, "Amen." And the elders fell down and worshiped. (Rev. 5:8-14)

I hope that John's unique access into heaven clears up whether or not our eternal home is going to be anthropocentric (man-centered) or theocentric (God-centered). Certainly we are the beneficiaries of such a wonderful place (along with angels), but our focus (as theirs) will be on God the Father (Rev. 5:13), God the Son (Rev. 7:10), and God the Holy Spirit, as he is an eternal part of the Trinity as well.

Myth: Heaven will be boring because all we will do is sing. I grew up surrounded by music. If the radio wasn't blasting the latest pop song, it was because someone was in the living room playing our upright piano. My mother was our church organist for years, my father would break out his alto saxophone from time to time, and my brother starred in a local band (today he is an accomplished guitar player and songwriter). I've dabbled in a variety of instruments myself, and all of us love to sing. So I get excited when I read passages that confirm singing will be a part of my experience in heaven (Rev. 5:9–10, 15:3). I cannot wait to sing praises to my God and King with millions of other believers, all with our glorified voices!

But will we do more than sing in heaven? Several years ago, I remember being the guest at a church in town that had an hour of singing before the message. I hate to admit this, but at the forty-five-minute mark my voice and my legs were starting to give out! I thoroughly enjoyed being ushered into God's presence by excellent musicians and powerful lyrics, but I was also looking forward to learning more from the teaching of God's Word. We weren't created solely for singing—and I love to sing!

Singing will be a part of what we will experience in heaven. But there will be so much more. The saints of God will also be working, eating, and creating. We will be enjoying rich fellowship while learning, growing, and participating in heavenly activities. There will be awesome adventures and immense joy, all with people we know and love. And that's just a taste of what we can look forward to. Boring? I don't think so!

Did you know that the New Jerusalem, heaven's primary city, is measured at approximately fourteen hundred miles long by fourteen hundred miles wide by fourteen hundred miles high (Rev. 21:15–16)? And if you walked around the outskirts of heaven's primary city, it would have the same feel as if you walked from Phoenix, Arizona, to Montgomery, Alabama, to Grand Forks, North

Dakota, to Kennewick, Washington, and back down to Phoenix, Arizona. Now just imagine going on that adventure with people you love, in a place you love, surrounded by new and intriguing elements, smiling and laughing, feeling safer than you've ever felt, and more at peace than you've ever been. And that's walking around the New Jerusalem. Wait until you go inside! If you've been impressed with God's creativity here on earth, you are in for the experience of an eternity, my friend! All who enter in will never want to be anyplace else. The apostle Paul sums it up when he says, "For to me, to live is Christ, and to die is gain" (Phil. 1:21).

> *If you've been impressed with God's creativity here on earth, you are in for the experience of an eternity, my friend! All who enter in will never want to be anyplace else.*

Perhaps author Randy Alcorn best sums up what your experience will be like in heaven when he says,

So look out a window. Take a walk. Talk with your friend. Use your God-given skills to paint or draw or build a shed or write a book. But imagine it—all of it—in its original condition. The happy dog with the wagging tail, not the snarling beast, beaten and starved. The flowers unwilted, the grass undying, the blue sky without pollution. People smiling and joyful, not angry, depressed, and empty. If you're not in a particularly beautiful place, close your eyes and envision the most beautiful place you've ever been—complete with palm trees, raging rivers, jagged mountains, waterfalls, or snow drifts.

Think of friends or family members who loved Jesus and are with Him now. Picture them with you, walking together in this place. All of you have powerful bodies, stronger than those of an Olympic decathlete. You are laughing, playing, talking, reminiscing. You reach up to a tree to pick an apple or an orange. You take a bite. It's so sweet that it's startling. You've never tasted anything so good. Now you see someone coming toward you. It's Jesus, with a big smile on his face. You fall to your knees in worship. He pulls you up and embraces you.

At last, you're with the person you were made for, in the place you were made to be. Everywhere you go there will be new people and places to enjoy, new things to discover. What's that you smell? A feast. A party's ahead. And you're invited. There's exploration and work to be done—and you can't wait to get started.[12]

Myth: We become angels who stalk loved ones on earth.
The expressions of sympathy I received after the accident were numerous and very appreciated. I read each one with thankfulness because they reminded me how loved Leigh Ann was and how brokenhearted people were for me and the kids. Sympathies came in all shapes and sizes. Texts, emails, cards, meals, financial gifts, handmade items. One person even made a book featuring Leigh Ann.

But while the pain was immense, I continued to operate out of a biblical worldview. This meant I continued to see things the way I had been seeing them since I became a believer, through the lens of Scripture. And what I came to understand was there was a lot of misinformation about the afterlife being embraced under the banner of sympathy. As long as the note was heartfelt, or the card had pretty pictures of sunlight breaking through dark clouds, then the content would have to be accurate. The last thing you're going to do is disagree with a sympathy card or never show your kids a homemade book about their mother. But that's exactly what I did.

It was a beautiful book. Leigh Ann, now in heaven, was pictured as an angel. She had the loving responsibility of watching over me and the kids so we could be at peace knowing she was close by. The hand-drawn pictures were colorful, and I have no doubt the kids would have loved seeing themselves in a book. They might have even been comforted with this version of their mom's new reality. None of it was what had really happened though. In fact, that book stood in direct conflict with our holy huddle that took place minutes after learning of Leigh Ann's death, when I told the kids that Leigh Ann was in heaven and that we would see her again someday, but, in the meantime, we would have to do life on our own without her.

I tell my students they better get used to themselves because they will always be themselves! They will always be human beings and have the characteristics that go with being humans who have been redeemed, including being made in God's image (Gen. 1:26), having the pleasure of marrying and procreating (Gen. 1:28), being born with a sin nature (Rom. 3:23), having the opportunity to be forgiven (2 Cor. 5:21), and being named children of God (Gal. 4:7), friends of Jesus (John 15:15), and co-heirs with Christ (Rom. 8:17). Angels possess none of these characteristics. As Alcorn sums it up, "Death is a relocation of the same person from one place to another. The place changes, but the person remains the same... Angels are angels. Humans are humans."[13]

Please know that people who tell you that your spouse or child who has passed away are now angels watching over you do so with the best of intentions. And while it is comforting to think our loved ones are nearby experiencing life with us, perhaps another thought to bring us comfort is that our loved ones are alive and well, free from any suffering or pain, rejoicing and celebrating with millions of other saints in their heavenly home. They have not forgotten you. Rather, if you too know Jesus, they are waiting with great anticipation for your arrival.

> *Day 167: Last night as I was moving some books around, I found one of Leigh's nursing books. As I was putting it in its new location, I found a piece of her hair tucked between the pages. Just one strand. I've never stared at a piece of hair for so long. Whatever it could have or should have represented, last night that piece of hair said to me, "I'm still alive!" I was reminded in that moment that Leigh Ann not only has hair but she has a brand-new body and, of course, still has that beautiful smile, which she probably used a thousand times today in heaven. I haven't seen or touched or held Leigh for 167 days, but last night I was actually holding a piece of her. It was hard and yet so very good.*

Myth: Don't worry, we're still married in heaven.

Of course, one of the more popular questions Fraternity members will ask themselves is, *What will my relationship be like with my spouse in heaven?* And if they're really being honest, they'll also ask, *If I get remarried, what will heaven look like between myself and my two spouses?*

Shortly after the accident, three women who were Latter-day Saints (Mormons) knocked on my door to offer condolences. I decided to be a little mischievous. I have a decent working knowledge of LDS theology and am aware of the few similarities and many differences between Mormonism and Protestantism, including differences regarding marriage in the afterlife. Whereas LDS doctrine allows for marriages sealed on earth (marriage ceremonies that take place in an LDS temple) to continue for all eternity,[14] the Bible advocates for all earthly marriages to end upon death (Matt. 22:29–30; Rom. 7:2; 1 Cor. 7:39), with only one metaphorical marriage existing in heaven, that of Christ and the Church (2 Cor. 11:2; Eph. 5:25–33; Rev. 19:7–9). After sitting down and listening to these sweet women offer very sincere words of encouragement and hope, I decided to act with naivety and asked a loaded question: "If I do remarry, who will be my wife in heaven? Leigh Ann or my new wife?" Their response was both humorous and yet slightly unsatisfying. After a long, awkward pause, the older of the three ladies said, "Well, Greg, at times God is mysterious in his ways, and we will just have to wait and see." They could immediately sense I wasn't terribly impressed with their answer, as I stared at them with a confused look. We exchanged a few more awkward pleasantries, and then they departed.

I did feel a tinge of guilt for wanting to discuss theology when all they wanted to do was tell me they were sorry for my loss. But there was a part of me that really did want to know how LDS theology answered what I would think to be an obvious question. Certainly, I was not the first to think of that conundrum!

And though I was settled in my theology, I missed Leigh Ann so much that I was willing to loosen up my previous convictions if that meant Leigh Ann and I would resume our marriage in heaven.

Day 11: *Father, thank you for heaven where Leigh is and thank you that I will see her again. Please, I beg you that we would mean more to each other than just a couple of saints. I need to see her again and know she is my wife. May we be able to live in heaven together, worshipping our King.*

Part of my grieving was from the constant wondering about intimate relationships on earth and what the rendering will be in heaven. Admittedly, I have more questions than answers when it comes to the familial knowledge of loved ones in heaven and how that will be expressed. I often think about Malia and Leigh Ann. Most likely Malia will spend much more time on earth than Leigh Ann did (thirty-five years). I have wondered how an eighty-five-year-old woman will interact with her thirty-five-year-old mother, whom she knew for four years on earth? Or will they both appear to be the same age? Or something else entirely?

I'm sure you have questions about your marriage and family dynamics and how everything will play out in heaven. While I may have underwhelmed you with answers, I can encourage you with two truths: Our ultimate marriage is to our Bridegroom Jesus Christ, and our ultimate family will include all those who know Jesus, including earthly family members. As hard as it is to imagine, I promise every relational piece of the puzzle will fall perfectly into place in heaven, and we will be more than satisfied!

Connecting with Jesus

One question I enjoy asking my students is, Why didn't Jesus perform more miracles, especially ones including healing? There are several accounts in the Gospels that show Jesus healing people. But if you consider how many people he came into contact with compared to the number of people he healed, the percentage healed would be significantly low. In fact, it would be safe to say Jesus fed more hungry people than he healed hurting people. Why? Simply put, Jesus wasn't on a mission to heal people physically as much as he was on a mission to heal people spiritually.

> He said to them, "Let's go somewhere else to the towns nearby, so that I may also preach there; for this is why I came." (Mark 1:38)

> For the Son of Man has come to seek and to save that which was lost. (Luke 19:10)

Jesus most certainly cares for your broken bones and broken heart. Several times we read of Jesus being moved with compassion to stretch out his hand and offer the hurting relief (Mark 1:41; Matt. 14:14, 20:34). You have a High Priest who can "sympathize with your weakness" and do something about it (Heb. 4:15). But your physical and emotional well-being are secondary to the health of your soul.

In a chapter titled "Heavenly Hope," I thought it would be appropriate to make something explicitly clear. Not everyone will be going to heaven. And it is because I desperately want you to be in heaven that I share the following good news.

If you have not met Jesus in a personal way, I would like for you to consider doing just that. The "Roman Road" to the gospel is available for you, right now.

Romans 3:23: "For all have sinned and fall short of the glory of God."
The Greek word (Greek is the original language of the New Testament) for "all" is just that—*all*. Because of Adam and Eve's willful disobedience to God, every one of us has been born with a sin nature. And that sin nature, if we're being honest, is far more in control of our lives that we would ever admit. The apostle Paul nails it when he says, "For the good that I want, I do not do, but I practice the very evil that I do not want. But if I am doing the very thing I do not want, I am no longer the one doing it, but sin which dwells in me" (Rom. 7:19–20).

Romans 6:23: "For the wages of sin is death."
Death was never meant to be a part of the human experience. Adam and Eve enjoyed sinless fellowship with God in the Garden of Eden, and their evening walks together were meant to last forever. The idea was never for them to grow old, die, and then spend forever in heaven. They were in heaven. After the infamous fruit debacle, sin entered the world, and with it came death, physical and spiritual separation from God. A life spent willingly rejecting God will result in an eternity apart from him. This final un-resting place is hell.

Romans 5:8: "But God demonstrates His own love toward us, in that while we were still sinners, Christ died for us."
Many of my friends are Bible memory whizbangs. They grew up in households attending Awana programs where memorizing Bible verses ("Sword Drills") was commonplace. I did not have that experience, but even if I did, I'm confident I would not have won many Bible memory quizzes. But if I had to select one favorite verse that I have put to memory, it would have to be Romans 5:8. I refer to it as

the gospel in nineteen words. It has just about everything I believe God wants you to know about him and you. And I can't think of a better verse to share with you during your grief.

Contrary to popular thought, our sin did not put Jesus on the cross. Rather, it was the Father's love for sinful man that drove his Son to be crucified. How amazingly deep is God's love toward me! This truth compels me to consider two more truths: First, the payment that was required to satisfy the sinner's debt was enormously personal and painful for God. May we never forget that. Second, our value as sinners who are loved as much as we are loved cannot be matched even by all the wealth the world can offer. May we also never forget that.

Romans 10:9–10: "That if you confess with your mouth Jesus as Lord, and believe in your heart that God raised Him from the dead, you will be saved; for with the heart a person believes, resulting in righteousness, and with the mouth he confesses, resulting in salvation."

Friend, I can only tell you from experience that putting my faith in Christ has proven to be the primary factor in allowing me to move toward true healing after losing Leigh Ann. And so I view this passage as a prayer of thanksgiving. God is allowing us to participate in the most important event of our lives by acknowledging Jesus as Lord and believing he is no longer in the grave. When this is done with sincerity and faith becomes as real to you as the ground you walk on, the angels rejoice! One more sinner has had enough of living on top of the throne of his life and now wants a right relationship with his Creator.

As you have already heard me say, your grief is a journey. You may be just trying to make it through each day without having a complete breakdown. You may be wondering where you are going to find the strength to face tomorrow. And after reading this chapter, you may still want some time and space to consider the invitation to believe in Christ. While my hope is always for the good news to be received, I want you to know I understand. I say this in truth: God knows your pain and is ready when you are to receive you into his loving arms, where peace that surpasses your understanding will be your companion through your pain.

Chapter Eight

Mercy Moments

*Therefore, let us draw near with confidence to the throne
of grace, so that we may receive mercy and find grace
to help in time of need.*
—Hebrews 4:16

In our seasons of pain, it's easy to get sideways in our theology. We're in crisis mode. Our emotions are pinging at all-time highs and lows. We contemplate things we never have before—revenge, self-harm, the meaning of life, the existence of God. These usually aren't planned considerations. We don't sit down with our books from the theologians of old and decide to spend an afternoon debating the finer points of the ontological argument for God's existence. Rather, we come home from single-parent shopping with three kids for four hours in triple-digit weather only to discover that we can't put together a simple office chair, and, in our frustration, we can smell our six-year-old, who is running around the house leaving a distinct odor in his wake. And when we proceed with a "bend-over" check, he has what can only be described as a Hershey bar–sized accident wedged between his cheeks that requires a top-to-bottom shower.

You're probably sensing this story is too real to be concocted (and maybe too relatable, for which I'm sorry), and you would be right. This is how the evening played out on day 151. It was five months into losing my wife and, on that night, I was trying hard not to go down the proverbial rabbit hole. I wasn't considering the various scriptures that confirm the sovereignty of God, nor am I quoting Jeremiah 29:11, affirming that he has a plan for me. I'm hanging on by a thread and needing something good to happen that night. Here's the rest of that entry.

Day 151: Bailey finally got cleaned up, so we moved on to cleaning up the recent tornado that blew through our house from 5 p.m. to 8 p.m. Somewhere in the middle of putting away the Sorry game and making up the boys' beds (Sidebar: Caden's comforter only works with black sheets, which were on Bailey's bed. Of course, you can't just switch sheets. First you have to convince Bailey that he's not losing his black sheets but he's gaining some cool grey sheets. Then everything has to be washed, dried, etc.), I lifted up a short prayer to God for peace and perseverance. I was in need of finishing the night without any blowups, by the kids or me. And within fifteen minutes all the kids had brushed their teeth, changed their clothes, and were in bed, all without me having to ask them twice. We said our prayers and "I love yous," and that was it. No Q&A sessions, no begging to stay up later, no asking for more to eat/drink. Right

now, they're all sound asleep, and the house is quiet. And my
prayer was answered.
And God is so good.

As you read this chapter, I want to come close to you and remind you that God really is still good. Please don't shut the book or turn the page. Hear me out. I'm not, in any sense, trying to lessen your reality. Nor am I attempting to sound clichéd. I'm desperately wanting you to make it through this year in decent enough shape to move into the next. And what I knew to be a great help was to listen to people who would remind me of theological truths. At times, I wasn't ready (or willing) to hear what they had to say. But it didn't lessen the truth in the message. And what I need you to hear is God is merciful and good. "For I am the LORD your God who takes hold of your right hand and says to you, Do not fear; I will help you" (Isa. 41:13).

My mother "adopted" a student from Kenya several years ago through a missions' program. Through her years of support, she has become very close to Sammy and his wife, Gladys. A few months ago, the young couple unexpectedly lost their only child, Lucky, to a life-threatening virus. Lucky was one year old. For the past several weeks, our family has been meeting with Sammy and Gladys through Facebook Messenger. We listen to this godly couple experience their year 1, and it's heartbreaking. In one of our times together, I advised Sammy to begin writing down all of his experiences. When he questioned why, I told him, "Because you need to remember how good God was, even in your pain."

Day 144: *Dad: Good morning, Bailey.*

Bay: Morning, Dad.

Bay: Dad, now that Mommy's gone, I think I like you a lot better than I used to.

I would have never remembered this moment, nor the others I'll share in this chapter, had it not been for my journal. I will never forget the incredible pain, the nights of desperation, the feelings of anger. But I'm grateful that I can look back and see these mercy moments. Why? Because I'm reminded that God never stopped being good to me.

Some of you may still be resisting this message, questioning God's goodness because of your situation. If God were truly good, he would have never allowed your circumstances to unfold the way they did. You wouldn't be alone; you wouldn't have lost your loved one; you wouldn't be crying yourself to sleep every night. How could I insist you read an entire chapter on God's mercy and goodness? First, I empathize with your thoughts, as I've had many of those myself. But if you'll come with me for a few moments, we need to take a swim into the deep end of the theological pool so we can put a few thoughts together that will ultimately help us in our journey.

Mercy and goodness are best viewed in light of depravity. The metanarrative of the Bible can be told through the biblical stories of creation, fall, redemption, and restoration. We bring the good news of the Gospel (Matt. 28; Acts 1) by sharing with others all four "acts" of the metanarrative, which is that God created man; man sinned against his Creator; God chose to redeem man through his Son, Jesus; and man is restored in his relationship with God by the death and resurrection of Jesus. This all occurs because God in his mercy and goodness chose to redeem his depraved creation.

Sadly, today's culture holds self-love, self-admiration, and self-absorption in very high regard. There is not a great deal of room for the idea that one needs to die to self to experience the richness and fullness of God's mercy and goodness. In fact, challenging anyone's thoughts or actions on this topic of self-fulfillment is a fast pass to getting "canceled." But you will never understand God's grace, mercy, and goodness if you don't first understand and admit to your depravity.

Even in today's "woke" culture, these verses can still be found in Scripture:

> The heart is more deceitful than all else, and is desperately sick; who can understand it? (Jer. 17:9)

> Behold, I was brought forth in iniquity, and in sin my mother conceived me. (Ps. 51:5)

> Jesus answered them, "Truly, truly, I say to you, everyone who commits sin is the slave of sin." (John 8:34)

> As it is written, "There is none righteous, not even one; there is none who understands, there is none who seeks for God." (Rom. 3:10-11)

> For all have sinned and fall short of the glory of God. (Rom. 3:23)

> And you were dead in your trespasses and sins. (Eph. 2:1)

I would encourage you to read through the book of Judges to gain more insight into the wickedness of man. Though God acted with patience, forgiveness, and love, every chance the Israelites had, they took advantage of doing "evil in the sight of the Lord" (Judg. 2:11; 3:7, 12; 4:1; 6:1; 10:6; 13:1), mainly through worshipping false idols. And if, after reading through Judges, there is a temptation to think you wouldn't do what the Israelites did, consider the "false idols" you have in your life today. It is easy to focus your energy on family, work, and entertainment and put aside growing in a relationship with your Creator. Though these idols may look different from those of the Israelites, the net result is the same: Our heart connects to something other than God.

I write all of this simply to explain that God wants to shower you with his mercy and goodness even though we don't deserve any of it. And he does that in the little things like providing an easier bedtime routine for a stressed and exhausted single father. In those moments of mercy, I easily related to other authors who also found peace in God's goodness. Wayne Grudem, in his book *Bible Doctrine*, said it well: "God's mercy means God's goodness toward those in misery and distress. God's grace means God's goodness toward those who deserve punishment."[15] Even John Piper writes of being "dumbfounded" when he thinks of God singing over us (Zeph. 3:17): "It is almost too good to be true. He virtually breaks forth into song when he hits upon a new way to do me good."[16] Experiencing God's mercy in the midst of pain can be a place of immense rest for those who are grieving. I hope that the following entries serve as an encouragement of God's goodness.

Day 36: Wish I could say this is a new day, I'm up and ready and excited to see what lies ahead. Can't do that. But I can say this is the day that the Lord has made, I will rejoice and be glad in it. Rejoicing has become an inward feeling of confidence and security that God is in control of this day. He was in control on March 6 and is in control of today. Being glad in today doesn't mean trials won't exist. I think being glad means I have a right relationship with God. He's in control, he's the Creator, he's the Giver of good things. (As I write this, my three kids wake up, one at a time, and slowly make their way to the living room, coming over and giving me a big hug. He is the Giver of good things isn't he!)

Day 47: *Malia learned how to snap her fingers. This alone is fun to watch, but when she snaps and adds some shoulder dips and head bobs, it becomes something you have to stop and simply enjoy. I love her so much.*

Day 128: *"Rain, rain, go away..." Monsooned a little the other night. Right before kids were jumping in the shower/bath, Caden noticed it was pouring outside. When the rain hits our back porch it comes down in sheets, which makes for a fun place to both watch the rain and play in the rain. The kids chose the latter. What was going to be a mundane, ho-hum taking of baths and showers turned into three naked kids having a blast in the rain. You would've thought they'd never seen rain before. Dancing, handstands, screaming. All because water was falling from the sky. They were having so much fun, and I was soaking in every second.*

Day 136: *We welcomed my nephew into the world sometime after nine o'clock last night. Twenty inches or so, and a little over* *eight pounds. The boy is already a serious cutie! Caden had the closest guess to the baby's actual birth date, so he was the first to discover the baby's name. And after we had all gathered in the hospital room, Reagan (Leigh's sister) and her husband, Jaime, gave Caden the honor of announcing to us for the very first time, "Liam Gabriel Guzman!" Liam was named in honor of his aunt Leigh Ann. I can barely write that without crying.*

Day 314: *Malia had the opportunity to spend the afternoon/ evening with Grandma Peggy, so I took advantage of the day and made it a "boys' day/night out." Caden and I watched every second of the Steelers beating the Ravens. What a fun time it was to see my son get as excited as me! Then it was on to the mall for some shopping, eating, and playing. While we all continue to miss Leigh Ann (Bay made a toast "to Mommy" at dinner), it was a precious few hours walking around with the boys.*

Day 328: *As God has been good to me and has provided these past ten months, so he did again in my bedroom. Feeling pretty bad about how I handled our marriage, I happened to glance at Leigh's nightstand. For some reason I haven't cleaned it off, and so there lay on top two or three of her prayer journals. Shortly after she died, I read many of her entries but then put them down and haven't picked them up for months. I don't look at her side of the bed too often and forgot they were even there. And for no good reason I picked up the one that was on top and flipped to the entry that was marked what I thought was the date (January 26). I had my dates wrong and the date was actually January 27 (ironically, Leigh had made no entry for the 27th). This hap-*

pened to be a journal she kept several years ago when it was just her, me, and Caden. This is what I read: "What a tremendous blessing you have given me in Greg…"

I'm smart enough to know Leigh could have filled ten journals on how I could've been a better husband and better father. But God knew on that night I needed to hear from her that it wasn't all bad. That our marriage had just as many spectacular times as it did challenges. So he directed my eyes to "What a tremendous blessing you have given me in Greg…"

Tears flowed, and I'm not really sure how the rest of the night went other than my heart changing from deep regret to calm and content.

In my moment of need God showed up.

Day 363: *I do credit God, and God alone, for the strength of being able to get up each day this past year and live with some degree of hope. I thank him that there have been many bright moments during this year of grief. Last night I was able to spend a few hours with Malia at our church's "Daddy Daughter Dance." We had a fantastic evening of dressing up, professional pictures, and outdoor dancing to the sounds of Justin Bieber! It was a night I won't soon forget.*

Friend, you are in a difficult season. I'm guessing you didn't ask for it. You're suffering, and the pain is real. You've been initiated into the Unwanted Fraternity, and you're dying on the inside. You're feeling helpless and hopeless. You're looking at your circumstances, and you're angry because it shouldn't have happened to you.

Please hear me. I'm with you. I know the feeling. But perhaps the right approach isn't to look at the *pain* in our situation and ask, *Why me?* Rather, the right approach may be to see the *mercy* and *goodness* in our situation and ask, *Why me?* None of us deserve his goodness, but if we will humble ourselves and accept the circumstances we're in, he will provide mercy in our time of need. Remember, "The Lord's loving kindnesses indeed never cease, for His compassions never fail" (Lam. 3:22).

> *None of us deserve his goodness, but if we will humble ourselves and accept the circumstances we're in, he will provide mercy in our time of need.*

Connecting with Jesus

When asked to describe Jesus, one might use depictions including God, Son of God, Savior, Teacher, and Friend. When was the last time, when discussing Jesus, the attribute "good" came up in the conversation? Not that anyone would argue the goodness of Jesus. It just doesn't get as much press as God the Father being good. "Good Good Jesus" might not have been in the running for Chris Tomlin's now famous song "Good Good Father."

Yet, consider Jesus's own words in John chapter 10:

> I am the good shepherd; the good shepherd lays down His life for the sheep. He who is a hired hand, and not a shepherd, who is not the owner of the sheep, sees the wolf coming, and leaves the sheep and flees, and the wolf snatches them and scatters them. He flees because he is a hired hand and

> is not concerned about the sheep. I am the good shepherd,
> and I know My own and My own know Me, even as the Father
> knows Me and I know the Father; and I lay down My life for
> the sheep. (John 10:11-15)

Jesus could have simply, and accurately, declared himself as the Shepherd. So why does he purposefully insert the adjective "good" (not once but twice) to describe what kind of Shepherd he is? Let me offer you two reasons taken from the text.

Jesus is the Good Shepherd because a good shepherd opposes the wolf. At the risk of sounding oversimplistic, ultimately, there are but two groups of people on planet Earth: those whose names have been written in the Book of Life (believers) and those whose names have not (unbelievers). The Scriptures confidently proclaim that believers will spend forever in heaven when life on earth is over (Matt. 27:38; Phil. 1:21–23; 1 Cor. 2:9; 1 Thess. 4:17) and that heaven will be a good place (Rev. 19:9, 21:3–4). As a believer I try hard to "keep seeking the things above, where Christ is" (Col. 3:1), for that is what fuels me, knowing one day I shall be with every believer worshipping our God in a place that is pure joy (Rev. 5:11–13).

Until that day, believers are told what to expect during their time on earth. Yes, there are to be seasons of joy, peace, rest, happiness, and satisfaction. However, the overall expectation should be one of war. The apostle Peter proclaims that the enemy has set out to "devour" as many believers as he can (1 Pet. 5:8). The apostle Paul urges the believers to "put on the full armor of God" because "our struggle is not against flesh and blood, but against the rulers, against the powers, against the world forces of this darkness, against the spiritual forces of wickedness in the heavenly places" (Eph. 6:11–12).

Friend, can I suggest that your struggles are exactly what Satan wants? In fact, he wants you to struggle more, not less. He wants you to feel isolated, defeated, depressed, and angry. He wants to keep picking the proverbial scab so you feel despondent and dejected. The father of lies will not stop attacking until you breathe your last breath. He is relentless. In John 10:11–15, guess who the "wolf" is? Observe what he wants to do—*snatch* you from the Good Shepherd. The Greek word used for *snatch* (*harpazō*) communicated to the early readers that they were going to lose more times than they were going to win.[17]

This is why Jesus is our Good Shepherd—he opposes the wolf. He does this day and night. He opposes the wolf with the strength that only the Good Shepherd possesses. He opposes the wolf so much that he will lay down his life to protect his sheep. In other words, Jesus knows your pain, and he doesn't want anyone adding to it. He doesn't want you to live in despair. He wants you to be healed, which will take some time. So while you're tending to your wounds, he's at the front of the gate keeping watch. He's your Good Shepherd.

The second reason Jesus is the Good Shepherd is because a good shepherd goes deep. "I know My own and My own know Me, even as the Father knows Me and I know the Father; and I lay down My life for the sheep" (John 10:15). Don't miss the depth of the weight of this passage. Jesus is equating the depth of your relationship with him to his relationship with the Father. Amazing!

I'm writing this chapter at a local coffee shop, and I'm in earshot of two middle-aged men who have been talking for well over thirty minutes. From the sounds of things, they are believers (I think one is a pastor) and are friends. Their conversation has moved around from selling a house to the presidential election to church-related challenges. It's nice to know there are other Christians who take the time to have fellowship on a Thursday morning. And yet, I wonder if the conversation will go any deeper? Will they introduce struggles, fears, hopes? Will they confess struggles with their spouses? Will they open up about sin and the current battle they're facing? I certainly hope so. But, if they're like me, I doubt it. Why? Choose from any number of common reasons we use to not go deeper with one another. Praise God that our Good Shepherd doesn't stop at the surface!

I'm reminded of King David's proclamation of our Good Shepherd in Psalm 23, "The Lord is my Shepherd, I shall not want." As a believer you will never have to want to be deeply known. Your deepest thoughts, concerns, struggles, and challenges and your profound moments of joy, elation, and wonderment are precious to our God. He is very interested in knowing you at that level. Amazingly, God has the capacity to know every one of his sheep at that level. You never have to worry if God has the time or desire. This is what makes Christianity unlike any other religion, for it truly is, as the cliché goes, "a relationship not a religion."

The passage I began with in Lamentations has a couple of translations for part B of verse 22. It can read "for His compassions do not fail" (Lam. 3:22b, NASB), and it can read "His mercies never cease" (Lam. 3:22b, NLT). God is waiting for those mercy moments with you so that he can begin to pour out his mercies to you. The question for you is, Will you get to know Jesus at the same depth that he's wanting to get to know you? Will you allow him into your pain today? Will you weep in front of him? Will you share with him your fears of not knowing what lies ahead? Will you trust him with your messy life? He's the Good Shepherd who has laid down his life for you. Now might be a good time to put this book down and get real with Jesus. He's ready for you.

Chapter Nine

Wonderfully Messy

"For My thoughts are not your thoughts,
nor are your ways My ways," declares the Lord.
—Isaiah 55:8

One of the groups I enjoy teaching most at my Christian high school is the seniors. I have the privilege every year to slowly watch many aspects of a senior's life unfold: turning eighteen, playing a sport for the last time, visiting colleges, wondering what to do with a current boyfriend or girlfriend, and all of the special events designed just for graduates, such as senior prom, senior class trip, baccalaureate, and, of course, graduation. All of this takes place in real time, so you can imagine how often God's will is discussed. "What does God want me to do after high school?" "Does God want me to go to college?" "What major does God want me to pursue?" "Does God want me to marry my current boyfriend?" In other words, how can I discover God's will for my life?

I've always enjoyed helping teens discover answers to these significant questions, but after Leigh Ann was killed, I was the one searching for answers. Financially, our household income would remain the same. The kids would end up receiving Social Security benefits from Leigh Ann's work, which meant we would not have to move across town or change schools. I could continue to teach at the high school, and our day-to-day routines could remain relatively normal. My search for God's will was focused in the area of relationships.

What began to creep into my thoughts from time to time was the idea of remaining single versus getting remarried. I can't identify exactly when or how frequently these thoughts would surface. I don't have any journal entries in year 1 that would implicate me in considering life with another woman, but it would be misleading if I told you the thoughts never occurred. I have never stopped, and will never stop, loving Leigh Ann. But the reality of being suddenly single after having been married for so long caused me to question, from time to time, if there would ever be another time I would experience marriage again.

This brings me back to the essential question: How do you know God's will for your life? Perhaps I can help. Simply put, if whatever you're doing is bringing God glory, then you can move with confidence that you are accomplishing his will. God most certainly has a plan for each of his children, and he cares deeply about the important questions they're asking about their futures. But when my students want to know what college to attend, or what major to select, my answers seem rather anticlimactic. I advise them with the following ideas:

- Be in good standing with God (1 John 1:9).
- Be growing in sanctification, especially through reading his Word (2 Tim. 3:16).
- Pray, pray, pray (Phil. 4:6).
- Be open to the Spirit's wisdom (1 Cor. 2:1–10).
- Seek wise counsel (Prov. 15:22).
- Assess spiritual gifts, skill sets, and natural talents (1 Cor. 12).
- Make a pro/con list (Prov. 16:9; Luke 14:28).
- Make a decision!

> *Simply put, if whatever you're doing is bringing God glory, then you can move with confidence that you are accomplishing his will.*

I believe I'm in good standing when I tell you many Christians take this pathway to making decisions. So when a student has a choice between Arizona State University and Northern Arizona University, I advise them to go through the steps and then make a decision. If, along the way, the Holy Spirit chooses to impress upon that student a "leading" toward a particular school, wonderful! My encouragement is that the Holy Spirit isn't obligated, so we need not wait for that leading before making a decision. On the other hand, the Holy Spirit may "close doors" or "stir our spirit" to not go to a certain school. As long as we're walking closely with the Lord, we can assume that stirring was from the Spirit and act accordingly.

At forty-two years old, I had to apply this very thinking to my own life. I was into the second year of my new journey as a widower and single father when I started to truly consider if

God might have me pursue another attempt at marriage. There wasn't anything overtly moving me in either direction. Part of me was content with remaining single and staying busy raising three children. But another part of me wanted to know if I would ever romantically love someone again. Even more so, I began to long for my kids to have what was robbed of them—the nurture and love from a mother.

After working through the very same steps mentioned above and not seeing much movement, I remember having a few conversations that landed me on the side of pursuing another relationship. Out of the blue, a couple of Leigh Ann's close friends encouraged me to think about dating again. This meant something to me. At times in the Scriptures, we see God using people as his means to communicate his will to others (think of the prophets), and I took these conversations as a possible sign that I should move in that direction. Perhaps the greatest sign came from a conversation with Leigh Ann's mother, Peggy.

Peggy and Leigh Ann had an unbreakable bond as mother and daughter. They genuinely enjoyed each other's company. The older Leigh Ann got, the more that bond shifted from mother and daughter to friend and friend. Malia's birth in 2005 only solidified that connection. Leigh Ann would be at Grandma Peggy's house often, showing off her adorable daughter. I hope it's no surprise then to say that Leigh Ann's death impacted Peggy in ways none of us will ever understand.

That is why I was somewhat mystified when Peggy pulled me aside one day in that second year after the accident and told me that if I wanted to start thinking about dating again, I would have her blessing. Peggy knew I deeply loved Leigh Ann. But Peggy also

knew my current situation and had enough wisdom and selfless-
ness to understand what might be best for me and the kids would
be another wife and mother. It was then I began to grapple with
trying to seek and understand God's will for my current situation.

The idea of God having a sovereign will over your life can be a
bit difficult to grasp. In fact, God's sovereign will, most certainly, is
one of the most difficult truths for a believer to accept, especially in
a season of severe suffering. But consider the truth that if God isn't
in control of your circumstances, then he ceases to be defined as
God. Of course, this idea is contrary to what the Scriptures declare.

> The Lord has established His throne in the heavens, And His
> sovereignty rules over all. (Ps. 103:19)

> Remember the former things long past, for I am God, and there
> is no other; I am God, and there is no one like Me, declaring the
> end from the beginning, and from ancient times things which
> have not been done, saying, "My plan will be established, and
> I will accomplish all My good pleasure." (Isa. 46:9-10)

> In Him we also have obtained an inheritance, having been
> predestined according to the purpose of Him who works all
> things in accordance with the plan of His will. (Eph. 1:11)

In the difficulty of embracing such a challenging truth, it is
sometimes helpful to consider the alternative. What if the event
that has caused you to pick up this book wasn't part of a bigger
plan? Would you be satisfied knowing your tragedy was the conclu-
sion of a random series of events? That God wasn't in control, and

your loved one was merely in the wrong place at the wrong time? Deep down, there is profound significance in applying Romans 8:28 to your tragedy: "And we know that God causes all things to work together for good to those who love God, to those who are called according to His purpose."

This idea of trusting in and agreeing with God's sovereign will has come painfully slow for me. You may recall earlier in the book I wanted to offer God my "plan B or at least raise suspicion on his plan A" (chapter 4). As I've interfaced with this concept, perhaps the reason "God's ways are not our ways" (Isa. 58) is in part because of time and space. God isn't bound by either, and because of that he is able to create our paths from beginning to end long before we enter the world. And with the exception of Mary, Joseph, and a few other women and men in the Bible, God does not reveal to us our future. For good reason.

I can't imagine what I would have thought had an angel showed up in 1986 in upstate New York and told my seventeen-year-old self that I would come to accept the Lord as my Savior; I would move to Arizona; I would experience indescribable happiness by marrying a beautiful, godly woman named Leigh Ann; I would then experience even greater happiness three separate times as she would give to me our three beautiful children; and then that our beautiful family would be destroyed through the selfish act of a stranger, which would bring unimaginable and unbearable pain, and at forty-one years old I would be initiated into the Unwanted Fraternity. But that's exactly how my story has unfolded. The awesome highs and the devastating lows. And I'm confident that if you're a member of the Fraternity, your story isn't what you would have imagined either. Additionally, if the Lord gives you another thirty days, thirty weeks, or thirty years, more change will come. When people say, "God's not through with you yet," what you need to hear is "God is going to accomplish his plans no matter what, and if you live long enough, that means more unexpected happenings will be coming your way. So get ready."

For some, what may be even more perplexing isn't the reality that your tragedy is included in God's sovereign will. Unlike my admission of doubting God, you're more at peace with the fact that the event has already happened and there's nothing you can do to change history. What keeps you up late into the night is wondering and worrying about the future. Your loss not only has caused you catastrophic pain, but it has wiped away foundational assumptions you had about your future. Questions that were easily answered prior to your tragedy are now looked at with eyes of puzzlement. Answers to where you live, what you do for your livelihood, who you're married to, and the number of children you have never caught you off guard before. Today they're all in a state of flux, which has you raising up cries to God with a desperate plea for answers. You're experiencing rich theology right in the middle of your prayers.

If the subject of God's will was not near to your heart, it is now. You need it to be if there is to be a future and a hope. This is where I landed when I decided to take Peggy's blessing and jump back into the dating scene.

Dating later in life is a trip! Everyone I've talked with who has been in a similar situation agrees there is nothing simple about the dating process. And the reality for middle-aged dating is not to wonder if someone is bringing baggage to the relationship; it's to wonder how much and how big the baggage. Then you have to embrace the feelings of being back in high school. Trying to decipher hidden meanings in text messages and constantly checking your phone, wondering if they'll ever call back (well, if you are my age, that looked more like awkward glances in the hallways and passing notes between classes). As well, you have the all too familiar nervous butterflies as you pull your minivan into their driveway ready to go on your first date.

My vehicle for helping to determine if dating was what I should be involved with was online dating. You may have your online dating platform of choice; mine was eHarmony. Admittedly the beginning weeks of this new adventure were diabolical! Setting up my profile was almost enough to make me want to quit the dating scene. I had forgotten what it was like to market oneself. I had been married for thirteen years and was dating Leigh Ann for two years prior, so I had been out of the game for fifteen years. What would I want to put on my profile? If I were honest, I would have put something like

> Widower (who still loves his wife), who wants some help with parenting three beautiful children. All of former wife's relatives live in town, so new person must be willing to spend lots of time with two dozen new family members. Widower doesn't make much money and owns two dogs.

Convinced I wouldn't get many takers with that approach, I scoured my camera roll for the most adventurous pictures I could find. And when my profile was eventually completed, anyone I got matched with would have seen pictures of me horseback riding (I did that once), running a Tough Mudder (I did that once), and golfing in Hawaii (I did that once). My profile told of a man who loved Jesus, was in fact a widower, and when not reading a good theological book or drinking his favorite coffee, loved taking adventures with his three adorable children. Come to find out, I wasn't the only one stretching the truth. I'm not being terribly hyperbolic when I tell you I had no idea every Christian woman also loves to read and drink coffee! Even more coincidentally, they also all enjoy running, listening to Beth Moore podcasts, and watching *Friends* or *The Office*.

With all the superficiality floating around, I simply had to bite the bullet and accept some of the matches to see if I could get to meet someone who was "God's will" material. And after several matches where God was clearly saying "Stay single," my inbox introduced me to "Jennifer, from Gilbert, AZ."

Admittedly Jennifer's profile was similar to most of the other female profiles. But there was something about Jennifer's eyes and smile that made me think she could be the real deal. After several weeks of online conversations, the moment came for me to take Jennifer on a first date. I wanted to play it cool and not suggest the clichéd dinner and movie, so I suggested spending a fun morning together of walking to a nearby lake and feeding the ducks. As Jennifer now tells the story, "That was so bizarre! I legitimately thought he got that from a horror movie, and now I was wondering if I should even go out with him!" Again, I had been out of the dating game for a long time!

We settled on coffee at 7:00 p.m. at Joe's Coffee House. Joe's closed at 9:00 p.m., so if the date was a bust for either party, there would only have to be two hours of suffering. I arrived ten minutes early and nervously waited for this woman I had only known through a website. Based on Jennifer's profile pictures, she was most definitely out of my league. But because pictures can be manipulated, I was hopeful but honestly didn't know what to expect. All to say, at seven o'clock one evening in January 2012, Jennifer O'Hara walked into that coffee shop looking for Greg Tonkinson. And our lives have never been the same.

How did I know it was God's will for me to marry Jennifer? Funny you should ask. As you'll soon find out, I didn't. Jennifer was so beautiful when she walked through the front door of Joe's, I literally couldn't believe she walked up to me and asked, "Are you Greg?" I've never been a part of the "A crowd," and here was an "A crowd" knockout talking to me! Jennifer and I instantly connected. In fact, we ended up closing down the coffee shop, so we headed to a wine bar and closed that down as well. That amazing first date led to several others, each better than the one before. We were intoxicated with each other from the very beginning. Maybe that's why neither of us knew what a colossal mistake it would be when I proposed just six weeks after that night at Joe's.

Infatuation can be an enormous blind spot for Unwanted Fraternity members. Jennifer had experienced her own devastating grief when her husband of twelve years walked out the door and left her and their two young boys. She came in brokenhearted and was still trying to pick up the pieces of a shattered self-esteem. After our first date, we discovered needs were being met; I was meeting her need for self-worth, and she was meeting my need for companionship. She was also loving on my kids in ways that made me think proposing was the right thing to do. So I asked her father, told my relatives, and even sought permission from my kids. Everyone was in favor, so we thought.

The proposal was something straight out of a movie. Jennifer came to my high school because I told her I was speaking for our weekly chapel. When she entered the darkened gym, she was greeted by hundreds of high school students all holding candles and red roses. As Jennifer shyly made her way to the stage, one of our students was singing a perfect rendition of "Come Away with Me" by Norah Jones, Jennifer's favorite artist. As the staff and students looked on, I bent my knee, publicly professed my love to Jennifer, and asked her to marry me. After she gladly accepted, we were whisked away in a stretch limousine, complete with champagne, to celebrate with our parents. And yes, we even stopped by Peggy's house, where she and Jennifer shared a beautiful hug. We were now scheduled to get married in four months.

With a little over a month before the big day, everything was getting finalized. It takes quite the effort to merge two families. I sold my house and my family moved in with Leigh Ann's parents while all of our belongings went to Jennifer's. We were establishing joint financial accounts, getting ready to change her last name, settling on honeymoon details (a first-class trip to Hawaii), and figuring out how to begin living as one big family. And then Thursday, April 26 happened.

If you recall the way I encouraged my students to make decisions, you may remember that number four on the list was "Be open to the Spirit's wisdom" (2 Cor. 2:10–12). While my theology bends more toward Reformed, I affirm the presence and power of the Holy Spirit and the numerous ways in which he works in believers' lives. And though the number of times I've felt the wisdom of the Spirit are few, I know with certainty one of those times was on Thursday, April 26. I vividly recall lying in bed that evening and being informed by the Spirit that I should not go through with the wedding.

Jennifer and I were infatuated with each other and had rushed things, as many couples do. We were pretty sure we loved each other, but we didn't let time get in the way of confirming that. We were merging two families, and we didn't take enough time to consider all of the ramifications of that enormous decision. So, after praying and knowing this wisdom was from the Lord, I drifted off to sleep with an incredible amount of peace. Of course, just because you know your decision is from the Lord, it doesn't soften the blow when you have to wake up the next morning and break off an engagement. I went to speak to Jennifer the next morning, and she had no idea what was coming.

It truly is a God thing that Jennifer and I are together today. Normally when an engagement is broken off, especially a month before the wedding, the damage is beyond repair. At times it certainly felt that way during our seven-hour conversation on Friday and our six-hour conversation on Saturday. Pain, anger, and shock were all a part of the discussion. As mentioned, Jennifer had already experienced abandonment, and now here I was ready to bring her that experience again. Though I knew what I was doing had to be done, I felt terrible (and still do) for putting Jennifer through that. She was so excited to begin a new season of life with me and my kids, and now I was asking her to entertain the thought that we might never get married. It was a torturous weekend.

Yet as the hours passed, both of us began to see some rays of hope. Saturday was just a little better than Friday, and Sunday was just a little better than Saturday. Jennifer told me that after thinking through things, there may have actually been some validity in postponing. There were still many issues we needed to work through, and the desire was to continue doing them as a dating couple. Late Saturday night we broke the news to our families. There were mixed reactions, but, overall, the families had a sense of understanding and support. That wasn't the case with everyone. Friends were understandably upset with my decision, and this led to many conversations that didn't end well.

With all my belongings at Jennifer's house, one can imagine how many things needed to be undone. I'll spare you all the details of moving trucks and storage units, but within a couple of weeks Jennifer and I were no longer planning a new life together. The kids and I moved into a townhouse, and though Jennifer and I tried dating off and on from time to time, we discovered there were too many emotions that prevented our relationship from getting serious again. We would end up spending the better part of four months doing life apart.

Oddly enough, at the same time we were apart, Jennifer and I both still sought God's will to be done in our relationship. Though there was fractured trust, a remnant of love remained that neither of us could shake. And just like the Holy Spirit spoke to me that day in April, I'll never forget the wisdom I received one afternoon in September. But I'm getting ahead of myself.

We had been apart for about three months, trying to maneuver through sporadic dating and phone calls. It was then that Jennifer sent me a gentle but firm email telling me that she simply couldn't deal with an on-again, off-again status any longer. The pain of not knowing where our relationship was headed was too great. Therefore she told me that we were officially over and that I should not speak to her ever again. My heart was broken, because Jennifer was only the second woman I had ever loved. I lost Leigh Ann in 2010, and now I was losing Jennifer.

I was able to survive nineteen days after that email without talking to the woman to whom I used to be engaged. But on that nineteenth day, I believe I received more wisdom from the Spirit impressing me to make things right. I jumped in my van and drove over to Jennifer's house with the same peace I had back in April. With ring in hand (she had given me back her ring) I reached her doorstep, rang the bell, and stood in her doorway telling her that I was now ready to love her the way she deserved to be loved. I showed her the ring and told her I would be willing to drive to Vegas that night if she wanted. It was then that she knew this was for real.

We didn't go to Vegas that night. We took our time and dated for another fourteen months. Somewhere in that time I re-proposed, at her house! Flower petals from the garage to the kitchen, Norah Jones on Alexa, and her ring on the dining room table. After she re-accepted, we drove to Sonic, ate hot dogs, and then caught the last few innings of the Yankees game back at her house. It was pure and sweet!

Jennifer and I were happily married before family and friends on December 28, 2013.

As I penned this chapter, I wanted to be extremely sensitive to the reader. You may read this and become skeptical, believing the only reason I've written about topics like God's goodness is because he provided for me another wife. Or you're in pain and this chapter added to your pain because you can't see life getting better. Makes sense why you would think that. Who wouldn't? That is precisely why I titled this chapter "Wonderfully Messy." I hope to dispel any wayward thinking that because I got remarried, my days of grief and pain have ended.

Rather, my desire is to promote a belief that if you live according to God's will for your life, you will find yourself in a continued paradox of rich blessings and unmistakable struggles. Certainly my blessings and struggles today are different from what they were ten years ago, but they are no less real. Today they are centered around my new reality of being remarried and raising a blended family. In fact, so vivid are the highs and lows of the past seven years that I sometimes wonder if I should write another book, along with my wife, Jennifer, of lessons learned from our time together raising our five children. We shall see!

Connecting with Jesus

Jesus knew the story from the beginning. He didn't wake up one day to the reality that he was the Messiah. When Jesus was twelve years old, reasoning with the teachers in the temple, he knew he would be the One who would atone for our sins (Luke 2:46). Jesus also knew his day-to-day agenda during his ministry years. He never woke up and wondered what the day would hold. He was never caught off guard, never confused, never in need of directions. Yet Jesus's life was messy! Not the messy you and I tend to think of when we say our lives are a mess. Our lives are often messy due to our poor choices. Rather, Jesus's life was messy because he was ministering to messy people. This is clear from three brief chapters in the Gospel of Mark (chapters 4–6), when Jesus encountered faithless disciples, a demon-possessed man, angry herdsmen, a distraught father, a chronically ill woman, skeptical childhood friends, five thousand hungry souls, and throngs of pallet-bound paralytics. Messy! But Jesus had help.

It's strange to think that Jesus would be in need of the Holy Spirit. After all, a trinitarian monotheist (one who believes in the biblical Trinity) readily embraces the fact that all three Personas of the Trinity are God. Yet Jesus was unique because of his humanness (Phil. 2:7), and therefore it is entirely plausible to understand that in the same way the Holy Spirit ministers to us, he did so with Christ. One might even imagine the Holy Spirit adoring the years he communed with Jesus during Jesus's earthly ministry.

I cannot say it better than Mark Jones when he writes,

> Christ's inseparable companion during his earthly ministry as a true man was the Holy Spirit. Therefore, at all of the major events in the life of Christ, the Holy Spirit took a prominent role. The Holy Spirit was the immediate, divine, efficient cause of the incarnation (Matt. 1:18, 20; Luke 1:35). This was a fitting "beginning" for Christ since Isaiah spoke of the Messiah as one endowed with the Spirit (Isa. 42:1, 61:1).[18]

Certainly, we must take our cue from Jesus and allow the Spirit to do the work in us he promises to do. When we arrive at the understanding, as I did, that God is for me, he does have a sovereign will, and he desires to live in a relationship with me through this "wonderfully messy" life, then a sense of "you are not alone" really does become a comforting reality. I encourage you to lean into that relationship with God and allow him to show you how to be in his plan in the midst of your current circumstances. He gets your "messy" far better than anyone else can. Trust him.

Chapter Ten

The Kids

Rejoice, young man, during your childhood, and let your heart be pleasant during the days of young manhood.
—Ecclesiastes 11:9

Whether you are on day 2 or 200 of your lifetime membership in the Unwanted Fraternity, you are keenly aware of how many people have been affected by your tragedy. Relatives, friends, coworkers, and neighbors are working through their own grief in their own way. Just like you, they didn't plan for this, and just like you they're experiencing loss with an unsurety of what tomorrow will bring. We empathize and do our best to understand, with full transparency that each of our journeys will end up being our own.

Over the past decade I have talked with hundreds about their losses. I've listened to heart-wrenching stories, some comparable to Job of the Bible, and I've cried a thousand tears, usually accompanied with a thousand prayers for God to heal the brokenness. The conversations are never ones I've looked forward to but always ones I'm glad I've had as I've watched hearts begin to heal right before my eyes. In between the weeping have been deep sighs of relief, as if the conversation provided an ever-small degree of hope, proving that life isn't over and that healing, while unhurried, can and will be a part of this journey.

One collective I had never formally sat down with to discuss the accident were my three children, Caden, Bailey, and Malia. Of course, we spent every day together in the years that followed. And even today, Bailey and Malia not only live with me, but they attend the school where I teach, so I'm able to see them more than most parents see their teenage children. Caden is out of the house, but we talk most every day and see each other once or twice a week. I like to think my relationship with my children could be classified as healthy. And yet, we've never had "the talk" until now.

Unlike some who have experienced loss, Leigh Ann's death has never been a taboo topic. The kids and I make it a point to include her in as much of our lives as possible. As previously mentioned, immediately after her passing, we established a weekly routine of visiting her grave. There, we would talk about Mom, remember the ways she loved each of us, and wonder out loud about her new heavenly abode. At home, except for her personal belongings, things stayed put. The way she decorated each room remained the same, the family pictures continued to hang on the walls, and the kids and I worked hard to maintain a similar set of house rules to those Leigh created. Keep the house clean, but life is more than a clean house!

Why the four of us never had a group discussion about the accident escapes me. Perhaps I didn't want to put the kids through the nightmare of recounting horrific memories. Or perhaps we were so focused on just getting through each day that the thought of sitting down and diving deep into what happened and how we were coping just didn't seem necessary. And while I am not a certified counselor, perhaps I concluded in those early years that because the classic signs of acting out, depression, being recluse, or a sharp decline in grades weren't present, that formal, lengthy discussions weren't necessary. Looking back, perhaps that could have been better thought through.

I knew I wanted to include a chapter in the book that focused on Leigh Ann's death through the eyes of her children. This is for two primary reasons: First, I've read numerous books on loss and grief and haven't seen many (if any) that dedicate an entire chapter to what the experience was like for the children. Yet part of my daily struggle, especially in the first year, was laboring over what the kids were experiencing, what they were feeling, how they were processing what was happening, and whether or not they were going to be OK. It would have been helpful to have heard from other parents with young children about what the kids went through, what worked, and what they would have changed.

> *I've read numerous books on loss and grief and haven't seen many (if any) that dedicate an entire chapter to what the experience was like for the children.*

Second, I am in a unique position because my kids are now older and are able to more clearly reflect on what they experienced ten years ago. My hope is that this chapter will provide some anecdotal insight that proves helpful to anyone in a similar situation.

This chapter is unique in format. It has to be. If I want to be true to the reasoning stated for writing this chapter, then it would be reasonable for you to hear directly from the kids without my commentary. Therefore, the remainder of this chapter will be the transcript of an interview that took place with Caden, Bailey, and Malia. The four of us recently gathered at a local hotel to specifically talk about the accident. I won't include the entire discussion, as we talked (and cried) for more than an hour. I'll provide what I think will be most helpful.

The Accident

Greg: OK, let's go back to March 6, 2010. It was a Saturday night. Tell me what you recall about that evening prior to the knock on the door. Let's start with you, Malia. You were four years old at the time. Do you remember anything prior to the police coming?

Malia: No.

Greg: Do you remember what you were doing or thinking?

Malia: No.

Greg: Bailey, what about you? You were six years old.

Bailey: I remember that we were all waiting for Mom to come home and she was running fairly late.

Greg: Caden, you are the oldest, you were ten years old. What do you remember if anything?

Caden: I remember that day pretty clearly. Mom was at work, and the four of us went to a little school fair in the morning. I remember playing with neighborhood friends in the afternoon and ripping my shirt. I came to you to ask what to do about it. You said I'd have to wait until Mom got home to fix it. Then I remember staying up a little later than usual to wait for Mom to come home.

Greg: It was about 9:30 p.m. when we got the knock on the door. So, the police came in, [and] you guys were in another part of the house.

Bailey: I remember I was in the family room sitting on the couches. I heard you scream like I never had. I remember really thinking that Daddy got a big shot, like a medical shot, because that's how I would scream for those. So, I just remember hoping you were OK from your shot.

Caden: I remember seeing the police and knowing that it had something to do with Mom. I remember running into my room and grabbing my pillow and putting my head in my pillow and praying to God. I was asking God for Mom to be all right, that Mom is doing good. Then I remember coming out to the living room and seeing you standing and then collapsing to the floor. I walked out and saw you collapse and I couldn't comprehend what was happening. Then you said, "Mommy was in an accident tonight and now she's in heaven."

Greg: We had our "holy huddle," and then I told you that a bunch of family and friends were going to come over. Do you remember that?

Caden: Yeah, I remember the whole night.

Malia: I remember before everyone came over, I talked to a childcare worker and she went with me to find Bailey's blanket that he lost in his closet. We went in his closet to find the blanket, and then we picked out a game and I watched them play it.

Bailey: That's right. I remember not being fully aware of the severity of what happened and thinking, *Why was everyone going to come over?* But I remember playing Connect Four with the childcare worker who came with the police.

Caden: I remember everyone coming over and just feeling so out of place because it was getting late and all these people were coming into the house. I guess I was in shock because I wasn't very emotional, but everyone else was. Grandma Peggy held me really tightly as she wept. She just held me and cried, and it felt like forever. I still wasn't putting it all together, so it was uncomfortable. All of our family and friends, like thirty people, were there, and it was a weird juxtaposition because usually we were all together for a happy occasion. But this time no one was happy.

The Viewing and the Funeral

Greg: Yeah, best as I can recall to my journals, people were there well into the morning. Various rooms had various emotions, anger for sure, confusion, we still didn't know all the details. Do you remember the week that followed up to the viewing and the funeral itself?

Caden: Mom died on a Saturday night, and we had her viewing the following Thursday. And I remember actually getting very excited for Thursday because I would get to see my mom again. But when I got there and actually saw her, I realized, even at ten years old, that it just wasn't her. I remember the smell of embalming fluid, that smell. I still remember it to this day. If I smell something similar, it brings me back, which sucks. I remember touching her hand, and it was cold. And I didn't think the makeup job was all that great. Just everything about that night confirmed that Mom wasn't on earth any longer.

Malia: I remember going up the casket holding your hand, Dad. It was just the four of us. Everyone else was outside the room. And then I ran to Grandma Peggy and she just held me.

Bailey: Yeah, I also remember holding Mom's hand and thinking it was stiff and cold. That's when, for me, it set in, that this is really happening.

Greg: Ten, six, and four years old. Do you remember the funeral at all?

Caden: I remember the funeral was beautiful with what everyone was saying about Mom. And I was processing all of it but not emotionally. We went from the church to the gravesite, and I remember standing at the casket when it was being lowered into the ground and not crying.

Greg: Why not cry?

Caden: I saw all my friends staring at me. So all I could think was *Don't cry*.

Single Parenting

Greg: Then we began our journey with just the four of us. Talk to me a little bit about what you recall in 2010, 2011, 2012, when it was just the four of us. Were you scared? Were you angry? Were you confused? What were you feeling during those two years immediately following Mom's death?

Malia: For me, I feel like I was emotionless during those years. I was just so confused.

Bailey: Yeah, same for me, lots of confusion. There was such a big hole in our house. I remember closely watching you as a dad, a single father, trying to figure out how the heck to do this new family life. When Mom was there, you never had to cook meals for the family, and now you were managing that by yourself. You never had to be the primary one to get us ready and take us to school. I especially remember you letting me and Malia dress ourselves. We picked out some crazy, stupid outfits! I remember constantly asking myself, *Why is this so hard?* And that hurt.

Malia: I also remember you trying to braid my hair. You really struggled with even just one braid! I think we moved to a side ponytail after that.

Caden: That switch you had to make didn't hit me until probably at high school. I guess I was able to gain a deeper perspective of all you were going through. Having to work full-time and then take care of us. If you were late in picking me up or if I had to walk home, I would get upset. But when I got older, I realized all you had to do just to keep things relatively sane.

Greg: What about how you handled the emotions?

Caden: For me, I was six months in before I started experiencing these waves of sadness and loneliness. It just sucked. Then, for another year or so, my emotional pain would turn physical. I'd be in my room, as a ten-year-old, writhing on the ground. This overarching question of why would hound me until I would break down and sob.

Greg: Where was I? Did I notice?

Caden: I remember mostly doing it in private. I remember you would come into my room once or twice and embrace me. And this was weird because I was thinking, *You're my dad, not my mom.* I wanted my mom, so it wasn't as comforting to me. Eventually I stopped telling you. I would just try to deal with it myself. Then over the course of like two years, those episodes would get less frequent and less painful. Probably the greatest thing was one day I stopped feeling anger toward the kid who killed Mom. I only had a small depth of Bible knowledge, but what I had, I would cling to. I would read Psalm 23 or something familiar to me, and I would find so much comfort and peace. So I would still ask God the "why" question, but I wasn't blaming him. And I would end up experiencing emotional and physical comfort, and that was so cool.

Greg: You were doing this on your own, as a preteen?

Caden: I guess so.

Greg: I never knew. Did any of you feel different around other kids because they had two parents and you didn't?

Bailey: For me it was pretty extreme, especially with the neighbors that we were close with, seeing their moms. Even now, seeing my friend's biological moms that they've grown up with since they were babies reminds me of what I lost.

Malia: When I was younger, I didn't really recognize that. But as I have gotten older, my friends would tell me about these close relationships they have with their moms. I will never experience that with my biological mother. It's hard sometimes when something triggers those thoughts about me and Mom.

Greg: Well, my next question…It's been ten years. Do you think that from such a catastrophic event you are emotionally in a good place? If so, how did you get there?

Malia: I do think I'm doing OK emotionally. But I'm also starting to discover things about Mom as I grow older, and those discoveries bring about a new wave of emotions. For instance, when I see pictures, I'm like, she has the same eyes as me. That reminds me that I never really knew this woman who is my mother. Also, the biggest struggle emotionally is if my stepmom has a rough day or is tired or gets mad at me, it can trigger some emotions. But I don't really get mad emotionally and think, *God, why did you do this?* I just ask God if he can just put my mom back here for one hour or so.

Greg: People have said that you all handled the death of Mom differently. Malia, they say that you closed off your emotions, where even today you don't cry a lot; you laugh a lot. But do you think that's a part of it, or is that a defense mechanism? You're pretty even-keeled, and you like to be happy and positive. But you're not ultradramatic with your personality. Do you think that had anything to do with it?

Malia: I think it did have something to do with it. I like to boil up all my emotions, and then sometimes I'll just let them all out. But most of the time, I like to be happy and joyful around other people so they don't see my true pain or whatever, if I'm dealing with it during that time. But then sometimes at night when I'm alone, I'll just cry about stuff.

Bailey: Malia, I remember at the cemetery you would say, "Why do you guys cry so much over there? I don't cry at all."

Malia: Yeah, whenever I'm at the cemetery, I try to forget about all that happened to Mom.

Caden: I think I could use therapy today. Not necessarily because of the accident. More so because of being raised by only a father for a number of years, for like my puberty years of ten to fourteen really, honestly. I remember in high school I flaunted how emotionless I was. I knew girls would just think I didn't have any emotions, and I felt so edgy. There is some undoing that I think could make me a little bit more empathetic to the human experience.

Greg: Do you guys remember any events you've gone through where you thought, *I love what's happening, but it also feels a little bittersweet?*

Caden: Yeah. Mostly near the end of high school, every accomplishment that I would do, through either singing or the all-state choir or graduating or anything, the thought would come up for sure, at least once, that Mom was not there to see me. This brought varying degrees of sadness.

Bailey: To me, it happens fairly frequently now, like Caden is saying towards his latter years of high school. That's where I'm at now, as I grow into more of an adult. Stuff like getting my license or just the big accomplishments in a teenager's life have really been hard for me. Even down to the smallest things like playing a sport, because it hurts to know Mom doesn't know what I've grown into, who I've become, whether it be good or bad. The mistakes I'm making and the accomplishments I'm making, she isn't on earth to see that or experience it with me, which really hurts.

Malia: For me, it was eighth grade graduation day. I was at my friend's house a couple days after that or before that, I can't remember which one. Then I just started crying and my friends were like, "What's wrong?" I said, "My mom won't be able to watch me go through high school and see me graduate eighth grade." So I feel like that was probably one of the biggest moments. I felt like she wouldn't see or do that. But there'll probably be more to come as I go through high school, especially not knowing what she did in high school and what sports she played. Getting to hear all the stories that the grandparents or you tell me about her during high school. It doesn't make me sadder but just makes me wish she was there to watch me play or do the same thing that she did in high school.

Caden: Another thing that kind is of off-topic. But in the latter years of high school/early college around eighteen, nineteen, I noticed that while the periods of intense pain had stopped, other deeper feelings had surfaced and a whole new revelation started. Where I started to forget. Things like I couldn't remember what my mom's voice sounded like or I couldn't picture what she wholly looked like or how she acted. When I started to lose that memory, it resurfaced a lot of stuff. That caused a whole another period of sadness.

Dating and Remarriage

Greg: So we have these moments where you guys are just trying to be kids, I'm just trying to be a dad. But you have school; I have work. So we kind of get into our rhythm and routine, and then in 2012 you find out that there's this person I'm interested in. Her name is Jennifer. We're going to do another book, Jennifer and I, on blended families. It'll probably be in the fiction/horror section. So I don't want to dive way deep into that. But it is a part of this story, and I just want to get a kid's perspective. So, Caden, you're now about twelve, Bailey you're about eight, Malia you're about six. What emotions did you have, and what was your perspective? Was there any anger because I was being bad to Mom, or was there a feeling of betrayal? Were you happy because now, finally, he can get some help? Just give us a little brief synopsis of that period of time when Jennifer and I started dating.

Malia: I feel like for me, I remember we were all in our rooms, and then you called us out into the living room. I was thinking, at first, I was going to get in trouble. Then I go into the living room and you said, "I met this girl." I can't remember exactly, but something about like "I met this girl." Yeah, I really can't remember that part. Then

I just remember thinking, *a new person*, and not really caring. Definitely, I really didn't care; I was just living life.

Bailey: I felt like it was soon. But I remember that when you guys were dating, Zack and Luke, our now stepbrothers, were spending a lot of time with us and were constantly begging for sleepovers. They'd come over to our house or we'd go over to their house, and we were best friends. It was a fun time to see you get married again and have a wife. But also having your best friends move in with you, the people you beg to sleep over every night, that now you may not beg to sleep over every night because they live with you. But I remember a lot of feelings of people telling me that God has always had a plan and that this was the end of the plan. They would say basically that this is the resolution to why your mom passed away because look how blessed you are now. To me, that was just a statement that made me bottle up all the emotions I had. These people were telling me that this fixes now what happened. Honestly, that made things a lot worse for me.

And it put Jen in a state of replacement, in my mind. Not because of anything you said or did but because of other people acting like she was replacing Mom in my life and in their lives. They were saying that this is why God did what he did and that was really painful, which now I have gotten over, having grown up a bit. But people saying that was not beneficial. As much as they were trying to be helpful or trying to make me feel better, it did not do that.

Caden: I remember crying, but it wasn't out of any emotion. I remember crying, and I wasn't sure why I was crying that you were seeing another person. I remember thinking it was kind of sort of happening fast. I remember just feeling kind of awkward. I think that whole period of like 2012 to '15 or '14, whenever that was, caught me in a great place. All I cared about during those years was myself, and Jen was friendly and wasn't intrusive. She had told me that she didn't want to be a replacement. So with those things, I was fine. I kept living my life as I wanted to because that's who I cared about. I was just dealing pretty unemotionally with the awkward changes of stepping into a blended family.

Malia: It's interesting to me now that I am older. I know a person who's in my grade and we're kind of friends. His mom died of cancer when he was little. I haven't really talked to him in-depth about it. But I know he's very emotional, and certain things will trigger him and he'll start crying in the middle of class. It's just interesting to see that and what he's gone through. His dad never remarried still and now he and his brother are just still living with his dad. It's just interesting with that and thinking about if you never got remarried. That would be us. But I'm starting to realize that I'm thankful that I have two parents now and not going through high school having one parent and experiencing that. I feel like that's extremely difficult getting older and older and just having one parent. So I'm always thankful for two, like now.

Wisdom for Other Youth

Greg: With that said, I have some final questions. To Malia's point, if you had to give other youth, from ages four to ten and even through twelve, thirteen years old, advice if they had just gone through something like this, what would you say? What advice would you give a kid who is in their first year of this or first month of this? Just let's stack the deck, let's say that their family knows Jesus and so we could start there. What would you say to that kid were the things that worked for you, things you wish you had done differently, things that you would tell the parent because of what you experienced? What would you do?

Caden: The first thing that comes to mind is I know what I wouldn't say to someone going through this. A lot of things people said to me were ignorant or hurtful. Bailey said something earlier, that people told him things like this happened for a reason. Things like, you'll see her again. For some reason, I still don't like that because I know when I get to heaven, I will see my mom, but our relationship won't be a mother-son relationship. It's hurtful because I will forever miss the relationship I could have had on this earth with her as my mom.

I know there are a lot of insensitive things people unknowingly say. My advice would probably be as a kid to not bottle up whatever you're feeling. It's not a kid's responsibility to bear everything that's going on. I think it's important for kids to talk to their parent about what's going on inside even if they can't find the perfect way to describe it. Bottling it up and trying to do it alone is just harder. It's as simple as communication. It makes it easier somehow. Just expressing what you're feeling, makes it easier somehow.

Bailey: My advice to someone in the similar age that I went through this with mainly would be first of all is this isn't going to leave you and it's not going to be over. But to always look to God through it. Like Caden was saying, the biggest thing to me that I wish I would have done, which led me down the path of not believing in God, would be to express your feelings with others. I know guys try to be tough and not emotional, but sharing your emotion is never a bad thing, especially when it comes to grief. I really, really wish I would have gone to my dad or grandparents, people who have more wisdom than I did, for answers to the questions I had. Those are the main things that caused me to doubt. So I wish I would have been more vocal about it and would have shared those emotions. Even to this day, I still struggle with that. I guess I feel like it's not masculine or that it'll make me look like lesser of a person because I have weaknesses as well. But I believe in sharing your grief. I know now you need to talk about those hard questions. Then to the parents raising the children alone. It's important to be there for the child even if it is in silence. The nights that I spent sleeping in the same bed as my dad were extremely helpful. Even though he didn't say much because I wasn't asking many things was good. But just having a person there is extremely helpful.

Malia: I feel like, for me, the bad thing I did was to bottle up my emotions instead of letting them all go. Especially at the cemetery. I would just be emotionless. I would not cry because it was easier to not think about the reality of it. I would tend to just forget about everything and think about what's going on tomorrow and stuff just to get my mind off of things. Something that has helped me get through some emotions is hanging out with my friends. Make sure you keep doing that.

Greg: Would you recommend counseling? If so, at what age when a kid loses their parents should they attend counseling?

Bailey: I think counseling is important, but I think a kid has to be able to recognize the tragedy that happened. I think for me it hit me around junior high. I think that would be a very important and pivotal time to have someone to share your emotions with. Without that, I felt that I was taught, especially being raised by a single father, to not show emotions. That's just how society plays it nowadays. But I think what's hard is you don't know where the kid is and they may not be ready to share emotions. I know I had a hardened heart at that time. So I think if you would have come to me and said, "Hey, we're going to get you counseling," I wouldn't have been very open to it. But depending on the situation, I very much think that those pivotal years through puberty are very good years to have counseling.

Caden: Yeah, I do agree. Yeah, counseling in fourth grade didn't help, but counseling in seventh and eighth probably would have. When I was in middle school and early high school, it would have probably helped. Yeah, puberty is a heck of a drug, saw some weird things come to my mind that I should have worked through but didn't really know how.

Closing Thoughts

Caden: My closing remarks would be I think a huge thing that I ponder often, that got us through, and it gets me through, is your and Jen's devotedness to faith and how that looks in life. I see in society today, just through social media, Twitter, and other people that their parents are as screwed up as they are, as these twenty-year-old college students that I know. They just don't have the Lord, and they're selfish and they'll do things that just don't make sense. I just didn't grow up not around that. I think a crucial thing about the health of our family and the transition is that Jen may not be perfect, but she loves the Lord. Paired with you, it just saves so much of a headache, of toxicity, and spiraling negativity, and bad habits, bad trends, all of that. So I would just applaud the two of for putting God first in your lives. I think for me, in my mind, the number one factor of why we are healthy is because you guys are healthy as humans in your faith. Where a lot of parents and people in their forties and fifties are not healthy. Then the other thing is I've grown a lot in the past year in empathy toward you as I've dated Nicole. She's slowly taking a place in my life, becoming one of the most important relationships I have. I can't imagine losing her, I can't imagine her death. Just to extrapolate that fifteen years down the road, I can't imagine what that would be like. So it's weird seeing these happy moments and then realizing that you went through them too. Meeting a girl and all that stuff.

Greg: I appreciate that, yeah. Thanks, Caden.

Bailey: I would say similar things as well. I don't think any of us would have worked out without a Christ-centered household and family structure. I wouldn't be where I'm at today whatsoever without Jesus, and I wouldn't be where I'm at with Jesus without you in my life and Jen as well. Having those influential role models that don't brag about what they're doing when it comes to the Word, but they show it through their actions. Walking downstairs at 4:30 a.m. and both of you sitting quietly with your Bibles open. Examples like that have led me to grow stronger in my faith. And like Caden said, I think growing up and going through our situation I was very ignorant and also very self-centered. I really didn't realize the severity of the situation. So that's something that I apologize for and thank you for always being there, never giving up. You could easily tell that you were us-centered. We were your number one priority besides God, down to my birthday party in the third grade at Amazing Jake's. When you invited the whole block and all my friends for me, and got a cool nice birthday party setup. Even though only the one kid we picked up showed up to that birthday party out of the twenty kids that were invited. You had a blast with me, Malia, and our neighbor. That was one of the biggest examples in my life. So it's a small example, but it's one of the biggest in my life that stuck with me, that showed how much you really cared for us, and I won't forget. I have pretty vague memories of Mom, which can be very discouraging at times. But I've heard so many different stories from people naming their kids after her or a nonprofit being named after her. She was a very special and unique person, especially in her faith, which gives me an even greater security of salvation. Knowing that I will be able to see her in heaven gives me great hope here on earth.

Malia: I agree. I don't know what else to say.

Greg: That's OK.

Malia: I know.

If you have children who are experiencing trauma, I'm certain you've spent sleepless nights agonizing over what lies ahead for them. If, somehow, you are able to put your head to the pillow for a few hours, you wake up and immediately begin to ruthlessly debate every decision you have to make on their behalf that day. You wonder if the times you chose to discipline will produce kids who hate you (and God), and if the times you chose to turn a blind eye will produce kids who act eerily familiar to the rebellious sons of Eli (1 Sam. 2).

Take heart, friend.

As I've wandered the halls of the Unwanted Fraternity for the past ten years, I've encountered many kindred souls, parents who are waking up every day hurting for their children. And as expected, no one has the answer to stop the hurt. We long for our children to be just that, children. We want them to grow up slowly, naturally, like most children. We want their biggest concerns to be whether or not they made the school play, or if they can make it across all the monkey bars at recess. We never wanted them spending their

Sunday afternoons looking at a gravestone while they contemplate where Mommy is now.

If the sit-down with my kids manifested any wisdom for parents who are looking for answers, perhaps they would include these points:

- Not understanding is normal.
- Crying and acting out is normal.
- Anger toward parents and God is normal.
- Counseling is highly recommended.
- What may be confusing in the moment will be understood later on.

Connecting with Jesus

Clearly Jesus had a soft spot in his heart for children. I would love to have been at Capernaum that day when his disciples were feverishly debating about who will be the greatest in the kingdom. You may recall Jesus's response: "And He called a child to Himself and set him among them, and said, 'Truly I say to you, unless you change and become like children, you will not enter the kingdom of heaven. So, whoever will humble himself like this child, he is the greatest in the kingdom of heaven'" (Matt. 18:1–5).

And while the disciples' focus may have still been on the question of greatness in the kingdom, Jesus drew the attention back to the child sitting on his lap: "And whoever receives one such child in My name, receives Me; but whoever causes one of these little ones who believe in Me to sin, it is better for him that a heavy millstone be hung around his neck, and that he be drowned in the depths of the sea" (Matt. 18:6–7).

It was almost as if Jesus was making two points: (1) answering the disciples' question, and (2) demonstrating how much he loved children. More notable is the account we read in Mark: "And they were bringing children to Him so that He would touch them; but the disciples rebuked them. But when Jesus saw this, He was indignant and said to them, 'Allow the children to come to Me; do not forbid them, for the kingdom of God belongs to such as these. Truly I say to you, whoever does not receive the kingdom of God like a child will not enter it at all.' And He took them in His arms and began blessing them, laying His hands on them" (Mark 9:13–16).

And if there is still any doubt, consider Matthew 9 when Jesus brings the official's deceased daughter back to life (Matt. 9:23–26).

Jesus in no way desires for your child to experience trauma. I do not see anywhere in Scripture where Jesus consoles Unwanted Fraternity children with the advice that their tragedy will make them stronger, or that their experience will draw them closer to God. If those things occur, praise God. But Jesus, like you, wants kids to be kids. And I have to imagine, like you, it pains him to see children who cry themselves to sleep.

> *Jesus in no way desires for your child to experience trauma. I do not see anywhere in Scripture where Jesus consoles Unwanted Fraternity children with the advice that their tragedy will make them stronger, or that their experience will draw them closer to God.*

Jesus truly does love the little children, all the children of the world.

Conclusion

But God demonstrates His love toward us,
in that while we were still sinners, Christ died for us.
—Romans 5:8

We've never met, but if I saw you having a drink at the pub in the Fraternity, I would buy the next round and say thanks. You began this journey with me at day 0. You allowed me to spend time with you during your darkest days. You sat shiva and listened to me as I poured out my heart. You cried with me and laughed with me, knowing I couldn't repay you the honor. I didn't deserve your empathy while you read my story, but you gave it anyway. Some of you have prayed for my wonderfully messy family. I now have some newfound Fraternity brothers and sisters to journey with until the Lord calls us home. I can't wait to meet some of you.

In the meantime I thought it would be fitting to conclude with day 365. Much like the rest of my journal entries, this entry doesn't provide as many answers as it does questions. I'm sure more copies would be sold if I titled this book *Seven Ways to Overcome Your Loss*, but all I really have is a profound experience that was captured in a journal. Perhaps some of you have been disappointed at the lack of deep biblical exposition. Clearly there are men and women who are far more versed in the Scriptures who can help you parse verses, argue doctrines, and satisfy your need to know the literary structures of the lament psalms. If that's you, I sincerely urge you to seek out their writings, as they will be good for your soul.

But if you've made it this far and there is a moderate amount of "I get you, Greg," then you are the one I wrote this for. I believe you and I would be friends because we know enough to know we don't know all that much. We're the ones in the Unwanted Fraternity, not necessarily looking for a way out but simply looking to talk with others who can relate to our immense pain. If that's you, then here I am. Friend, if you're on day 23 and you feel like there's no way out, hang in there. I'm on day 4,004. We're in this together. One Fraternity, several members.

> **Day 365:** *Last Friday I forecasted what yesterday might be like and in my "every now and then I make a good decision" wisdom I took off work today, kept the kids out of school, reserved a room at a local hotel for last night, and decided to do yesterday with just the four of us.*
>
> *By God's grace we had a wonderful time swimming, eating junk food, turning the room down to freezing, and jumping on the beds. But mostly we had time with each other. In the hot tub we played "name one thing you appreciate about each other."*

When it got to "one thing I appreciate about Mommy," the tears welled up, but that was par for the course yesterday.

A tremendously emotional day. My phone blew up with emails, texts, and calls. Very similar to day 1. You'd think it would've been overwhelming, but it turned out to be extremely comforting. People from around the world remembering Leigh Ann and expressing sympathy for me and the kids. When we arrived at the cemetery, we were greeted by three families all there to remember Leigh. Every Sunday the kids and I are there alone, so it was good to see others there and to grieve as a community. Leigh's death has broken the hearts of many, and yet there is something beautiful about living in pain together. In a weird way I loved hearing how others were having a rough day. Made me feel normal.

Yesterday I reflected on what this past year has brought to me and the kids, our families, our friends. Here are a few of things that came to mind:

- *I'm not alone in my pain. I've met dozens of people who could one-up me regarding pain. And though Leigh was my wife, she was also a daughter, mother, sister, aunt, coworker, and friend. We're all experiencing her loss. As well, everywhere I preached last year there was someone in the audience who could relate to my situation because they were in a situation of their own. Pain doesn't invite a few to the party. We're all invited.*

- *Our days are numbered. Death is coming and there is no escape.*

- *Seemingly there is no rhyme or reason as to how many days we're given. God knows but very seldom makes the* reason clear. The timing of Leigh's death continues to frustrate me, but I've also been confused at others' passing. Children, young adults, etc. For many of us there will always be a question mark as to why.

- God is mysterious. His ways are not my ways. I'm more confused about God than I've ever been.

- The Scriptures are both comforting and complicated. I've sensed God more this past year than ever before. His Word has fulfilled its promise of teaching me (2 Tim 3:16) great things about myself, life, heaven. Yet I've never had more questions than I do now. For instance:

  - Prayer is a mystery. Does prayer truly change things? Is God dependent on people's prayers for healing, provision, blessings? Is God's sovereign will affected by prayer? How come the answer to our prayers seems to be very random (God heals one person but not another though they were both equally prayed for)? Why do we tell people prayer works but when it doesn't we say, "God's answer was no?" Seems like a religious win-win without any way to disagree.

  - My purpose on earth isn't as clear as it used to be. Why was I created? To be tested as to whether I would respond to the gospel? We talk of purpose in terms of "knowing God and making him known," but that seems to make more sense when talking of someone who is older in age. What about the child who dies a painful death? What was their purpose? To say, "God only knows" again seems like a religious win-win.

- *My worship has never been more pure. My intimacy with God has been authentic. I care less about what others think, knowing God is my only audience. The words I sing have more meaning because I picture what Leigh is experiencing, and I'm left with the choice of either believing or not. I choose to believe.*
- *I live with a great deal of hope. I know that sounds contradictory to some things noted above, but somehow it's true. I believe heaven is just around the corner, and though I'm confused, I trust the Word. Jesus is there, Leigh is there, and heaven will be magnificent.*
- *God is good. My kids and I have been blessed by God this past year in indescribable ways. Though I'm confused by him, I'm also in awe of him. I've experienced his peace, his comfort, his healing, and his love in new ways this past year. Things only he could have done for me. I'm grateful he hasn't abandoned me in my darkest hour.*
- *I'm less bound by "stuff." If I need something, I'll ask you for it. If I have something you need, come and get it— seriously. This principle began because of the outpouring of support the kids and I have experienced. Meals, money, acts of service continue to come our way. We don't deserve any of it, and yet it keeps coming. And so I've tried to be proactive in giving. I'm not taking any of it with me, and there are so many in need. And to bring it down to everyday living, how fun is it to do something nice for someone? Try picking up the tab every now and then. It's hilariously fun.*

- *I'm in this for the long haul with my kids. Caden, Bailey, and Malia are mine, and though there are days we're not the best of friends, our relationship has forever changed. Our love for each other continues to drill down past what I've ever experienced with anyone sans Leigh Ann. This past year it's just been the four of us, and it's looking to be a repeat this year. This doesn't take away from the countless hours family and friends have invested in our lives. But at the end of the day the kids are my responsibility, and for now I'm up for the challenge.*

- *I'm less dependent on people and more dependent on Christ. I don't know if I'll remarry. I do know Jesus is all I need. Should he provide a helpmate, I won't fight it. But if that never happens, my identity will still be found in him. I'll still be whole and perfectly capable of living a successful life.*

All to say I'm launching into year 2 as a confused, imperfect father of three who is choosing to live by faith in the One who deserves my heart, mind, and soul.

One day at a time...

Acknowledgments

This section of the book was the most enjoyable to write. Wasn't even close. This is the time to pull back the curtain and proudly proclaim who stood in my corner and helped make the process of writing *Unwanted Fraternity* more rewarding than I deserve.

None of this happens without my wife Jennifer. Her encouragement early on and her unwavering commitment during the years it took to write the book are the only reasons I was able to complete the manuscript. She supported the countless hours I needed to focus on writing, which meant she had to manage our large family by herself. She was my early editor, and her suggestions remain invaluable. No one was closer to this material than Jennifer, and I owe her everything. I love you.

I'm grateful to Caden, Bailey, and Malia for giving me permission to share our story. It's as much theirs as it is mine. They've been through so much at such young ages, and it would have been fair to ask me not to put their lives on public display. But they share my passion to help other Fraternity members, especially when it involves children and teenagers. I love who God is making in each of them.

To my extended family members who ministered to me and the kids, especially during our first year in this journey. You rescued us in our greatest time of need. It took (and continually takes) a village to get three kids and a grieving widower from point A to point B every day, and you all did it (and do it) with unconditional love. I am indebted to a group who would never want to be paid back and so I can only say thank you.

To my friends who continually made the time to check in and make sure I was grieving well. The phone calls, emails, and texts were precious, and though there were times I was too busy or too tired to respond, I want you to know I needed to hear from each of you in those very moments. I'm particularly thankful for all the times you told me you were praying for me and the kids.

To my Valley Christian Schools (VCS) family. I will forever tell everyone that working at VCS when the accident occurred was most certainly a God-thing for my family. You grieved so well with me, allowing me as much time as needed to stay home, allowing me to leave midday if need be, coming to the house with more food than we knew what to do with, and loving on us because you cared deeply.

Thank you to Tom Dean for taking a chance on me and for recommending my work to the team at Morgan James Publishing. And to everyone at Morgan James who supported this effort. I'll always remember the feeling I had after our Mastermind call, one of unbridled joy that this book was actually going to become a reality. Throughout the publishing process, you seemed as excited as Jennifer and I did, and that meant the world to us.

The vast number of decisions one has to make when writing a book can be overwhelming. While some of my decisions can be called into question, one that I will stand by was the hiring of Amanda Rooker at Split Seed Media to work as my editor. Not only did Amanda provide an elite level of editing, but she demonstrated a clear understanding for the purpose of the book and thus gave it great care. Jennifer and I highly recommend Amanda.

It may seem as if I'm assigning far too much credit to individuals and not to God. I believe God knows that any applause offered above is to be understood through the lens that he has been at work through those people. Throughout this journey, the Lord continues to be my rock, my friend, my comfort, my healer, my Abba Father. And though I have often wandered from my desire to offer unceasing praise, may *Unwanted Fraternity* be an artifact that brings my King delight.

Notes

1   If you're experiencing loss, please read Jerry Sittser's book, *A Grace Disguised* (Grand Rapids, MI: Zondervan, 2004). It will most certainly help you in your journey of grief.

2   Lexico Online Dictionary, "Accident," accessed July 5, 2019, https://www.lexico.com/en/definition/accident.

3   Dan Allender, "The Hidden Hope in Lament," Allender Center at the Seattle School (website), June 2, 2016, accessed July 24, 2019, https://theallendercenter.org/2016/06/hidden-hope-lament.

4   Lesley Hazelton, *The Doubt Essential to Faith*, June 24, 2013, accessed July 24, 2019, https://www.youtube.com/watch?v=6ORDQFh0Byw.

5   Brennan Manning, *The Ragamuffin Gospel* (Colorado Springs: Multnomah, 2005), 40.

6   Harold Lindsell, *Harper Study Bible* (Grand Rapids, MI: Zondervan, 1985), 1497 (footnote to Philippians 2:7).

7   Max Lucado, *Just Like Jesus* (Nashville: Word, 1998), 136.

8   C. S. Lewis, *The Joyful Christian* (New York: Macmillan, 1977), 191.

9   John Piper, "Did Jesus Diminish His Divine Power to Become Human?" December 18, 2017, Desiring God: Ask Pastor John (website), https://www.desiringgod.org/interviews/did-jesus-diminish-his-divine-power-to-become-human.

10   M. Chave-Jones, "Loneliness," in *New Dictionary of Christian Ethics and Pastoral Theology*, ed. David J. Atkinson and David F. Field (Downers Grove, IL: InterVarsity, 1995), 556–557.

11   Hillsong, "What a Beautiful Name" (2017). Retrieved from https://www.worshiptogether.com/songs/what-a-beautiful-name-hillsong-worship.

12   Randy Alcorn, *Heaven: A Comprehensive Guide to Everything the Bible Says about Our Eternal Home* (Wheaton, IL: Tyndale House, 2004), 18.

13   Alcorn, *Heaven*, 275.

14   Spencer Kimball, "Celestial Marriage," Church of Jesus Christ of Latter-day Saints (website), accessed March 14, 2021, https://www.churchofjesuschrist.org/study/manual/doctrines-of-the-gospel-student-manual/28-celestial-marriage?lang=eng.

15   Wayne Grudem, *Bible Doctrine* (Grand Rapids, MI: Zondervan, 2014), 91.

16   John Piper, *The Pleasures of God* (New York: WaterBrook Multnomah, 2000), 180.

17   As William Mounce states, "As a general rule, harpazō underscores the power of the snatcher over the snatched." William D. Mounce, *Mounce's Complete Expository Dictionary*

of Old and New Testament Words (Grand Rapids, MI: Zondervan, 2006), 666.

18 Mark Jones, "Why Jesus Needed the Holy Spirit," March 12, 2019, Desiring God (website), accessed January 31, 2021, https://www.desiringgod.org/articles//why-jesus-needed-the-holy-spirit.

About the Author

D r. Greg Tonkinson currently serves as the Spiritual Life Director for Valley Christian Schools (Chandler, Arizona). He has served at VCS for fourteen years and has lived in the Phoenix area for thirty-six years. Prior to working in Christian education, Dr. Tonkinson served for over a decade in the local church as a church planter, teaching pastor, and worship pastor. Dr. Tonkinson is a TEDx speaker, has been a guest of Guy Raz (NPR), and proudly performed a forty-five-minute interview with President George W. Bush. Dr. Tonkinson received his MDiv from Phoenix Seminary (1998) and his DMin from Talbot School of Theology (2015). He is married to Jennifer and has five children.

A free ebook edition is available with the purchase of this book.

To claim your free ebook edition:

1. Visit MorganJamesBOGO.com
2. Sign your name CLEARLY in the space
3. Complete the form and submit a photo of the entire copyright page
4. You or your friend can download the ebook to your preferred device

Print & Digital Together Forever.

Snap a photo

Free ebook

Read anywhere

CPSIA information can be obtained
at www.ICGtesting.com
Printed in the USA
JSHW031815010722
27693JS00002B/2